THIRST
AFTER
G·O·D

DENIS·BALL

LESLIE PLAYER

Marshall Pickering

Marshall Morgan and Scott
Marshall Pickering
3 Beggarwood Lane, Basingstoke, Hants RG23 7LP, UK

British Library CIP Data
Ball, Denis
Thirst after God.
1. Christian Life – 1960
I. Title
248.4   BV4501.2
ISBN 0–551–01428–8

Text set in 10/11 Plantin by Input Typesetting Ltd, London
Printed in Great Britain by
Anchor Brendon Ltd, Tiptree, Essex.

Contents

Preface.

When two people fall in love it is the most natural thing in the world for them to want to be together. They don't consider it a hardship; how can they – they're in love!

God is deeply in love with His creation, including you and me, and His great heart yearns for our love-response. Too often we mistake serving God for loving Him, but true love for God arises from a genuine desire and willingness to be loved by Him. He will initiate the loving if we offer ourselves. As we give ourselves to discovering Him, to waiting on Him and to listening to Him, so He is able to reach out to us and draw us closer into His embrace. This closeness changes duty into delight and our eyes are gently opened to His beauty and worth. Worship and adoration flow naturally from the heart.

The Bible calls this holiness – the close walk with God. It is the path of true happiness; the natural Christian's way. Needless to say, it is a process lasting a lifetime. It takes time, practice and patience – but it's worth it!

This is very much a 'how to' book written in simple terms to help anyone grasp some of the essential truths of self-preparation which, in turn, can lead to a better appreciation of the practice of communion with God. In so doing, we are more disposed to receive His love and to offer Him our love-response. I have included some exercises to help stimulate a deeper God-awareness and longing for union with Him, and each chapter closes with a prayer should the reader desire to put into action what has been read.

Now that I've finished this book I realise how imperfectly I have treated such a great subject, but if it helps anyone who thirsts after God to draw a little closer to Him, I shall be reasonably happy. He is a God so worthy of our love and appreciation.

I feel I must place on record my sincere thanks to Florence Mary, my dear wife, who never ceased encouraging me, to David for his understanding presence, to Bill and Paula, the Sacred Dance Group and our long-suffering trustees, Reg, Lucia and Tony, who made sure I had the time and backing, and to Walter and Kathrin and my good friends at J.M.E.M., Biel, for their very practical support. Finally, I must tend my thanks to Debbie Thorpe of Marshall Pickering for chivying a reluctant writer to get started. Thank you to all who encouraged me.

1: The Way to the Father's Heart.

I once heard a young man pray, 'Oh Lord, please help me to love you more . . . you see Lord, I really do want to be holy for you.'

I remember the prayer well because it was a prayer I had often prayed – the prayer of desperation. And yet, it is a prayer of some significance for I have since come to realise that love and holiness walk hand in hand. To know the joy of a holy walk with God is only possible when we are certain that He really loves us. What, then, links the hand of holiness to the hand of love?

A new person – by faith.

St Thomas Aquinas, the great thirteenth-century theologian and philosopher, wrote this on the subject of faith in his Commentary on the Apostles' Creed.

> None of the philosophers before the coming of Christ could by bending all effort to the task know as much about God and the things necessary for eternal life as after the coming of Christ a little old woman knows through her faith.

What a remarkable statement this is. St Thomas is saying that this little old woman, although she is a nobody in the sight of the world, is a very special person. When it comes to knowing about God and things relating to eternal life she is superior to all the philosophers before Christ. And the reason? Why, through her faith in what this Christ has done on her behalf she has become a changed person – a new creation, in fact – and His Holy Spirit is living within her. The same may be said for every Christian. But this brings us back to the question, that if all this is true, how do we make holiness link hands with love? Why is it easier for some people to live more holy lives than others, and why do some love God more than others?

The central truth of the Cross.

There is, I think, a helpful answer and we may find it if we examine the accounts of the lives of holy men and women who have lived since Christ. They had no advantages over the little old woman but there was one truth they regarded as more precious than all others. It was the truth of God's unspeakable love for all people and His plan to restore them to Himself from their fallen condition through His Son's sacrifice. You will discover that all these holy people placed great importance on this theme, not simply as the entrance into the Kingdom of God but, especially, as the sustaining power for their daily lives.

If we read the writings of St Paul we shall see that he lays great stress on the cross and the crucified Lord. At the same time he looks upward and beyond to a Christ who has triumphed over sin and death, a Christ who is drawing us to Himself to bring satisfaction to his Father. To be honest, it is not a subject many Christians care to consider, let alone meditate on. We must remember that the cross is the place of encounter with God, of death to self, of transformation, the doorway to a life of God-awareness. I think that many of us know how to enter God's kingdom by that way but steer clear of it afterwards and leave untouched the many benefits that way has to help us grow.

St John of the Cross.

Recently, I was reviewing the life and work of the mystic St John of the Cross who lived in the sixteenth century. Of humble yet noble parents he entered a Carmelite monastery and later became a joint founder of the Discalced (unshod) Carmelites. Although he was rather small in stature and very retiring, he was not the kind of person we should want to cross swords with. He held very strong opinions on a number of religious matters which occasionally got him into trouble – he was even once imprisoned for nine months by his own brothers.

So, what is it that made him so famous; what has kept his name alive until today? Is it the life he lived? Not particularly, although it is an inspiration. Surely, it is his remarkable writings, especially his exquisite poetry and prose. Listen to two of the stanzas from his famous *Living Flame of Love*.

Oh, living flame of love that tenderly woundest my
soul in its deepest centre,
Since thou art no longer oppressive, perfect me now if
it be thy will. Break the web of this sweet surrender.

Oh, sweet burn! Oh, delectable wound! Oh, soft hand!
Oh, delicate touch,
That savours of eternal life and pays every debt! In
slaying, thou hast changed death into life.

Holy ground.

Now, what do you make of these beautiful lines; what do they say to you?

I found them deeply moving and poignant but it was some while before I began to understand them. However, what the first reading did for me was to trigger an unusual response – a response towards God. I felt that I was walking on holy ground; looking into the secret place of the soul of a man who knew things I did not know. With humbled heart I desired to look beyond what my natural senses told me, and if possible, see some very small part of what he saw.

Two questions arose in my mind. The first was, what had been revealed to him to effect such a transformation? The second was, what was this effect? Surely, the answers must be found in his writings. These are my very imperfect observations.

Sweet forgiveness.

While St John was not the most attractive looking of men he was humble and sought to follow the pathway of God's truth. It had meant much self-discipline and heart-searching but he had had the courage and the help of the saintly Teresa at Avila, who was the prioress of the Convent of the Incarnation where he was confessor.

St John had come to see that any valid relationship with God depended on him being fully committed to God – mind, body and spirit. It was much more than being committed to a cause or religious life. He had longed for a personal encounter with God, a fusion with God, but this was no simple matter. Time and again one important truth had become clear to him as he had sought to approach God. His sins had stood in the way.

The way I see it, the day of glorious revelation dawned when he stood before the crucified Lord to witness the terrifying struggle between life and death. As he gazed into the mangled face of his Saviour he saw no reproach yet he knew this bloody fight was on his behalf. No cries were heard; no bitter reviling for the task He alone could perform. Freely He had come to this dreadful place and freely He gave himself for such is the nature of true love. And from those parched, drawn lips St John heard the words his soul had thirsted for, 'My child, you are forgiven!'

Oh, delicate touch!

If I may pursue the matter to its conclusion I see a man now passionately in love, who not only understands the meaning and work of the Cross of Christ but joyfully embraces all the new obligations of fuller commitment and obedience. He is a man enraptured. But one thing more he must do; he must identify with this God made man who had so graciously sought to identify with him – a sinner. Overwhelmed by such compassion and sacrifice he reaches up with infinite tenderness to touch one of the nail-pierced hands. But to St John it is as if the hand of God Himself has reached out to him.

Oh, sweet burn! Oh, delectable wound! Oh, soft hand! Oh, delicate touch,
That savours of eternal life and pays every debt! In slaying, thou hast changed death into life.

Yes, we can say with reasonable certainty that St John understood the meaning and power of the Cross, that for him it was the only place where true holiness could be sustained through receiving its benefits by faith. In understanding this transforming work he had been released to a vitally new love relationship.

What about us?

I am sure that all this raises in our minds many pertinent questions, such as, should this be my experience too? Where, then, have I gone wrong? Does God have favourites like St John? Does He love some people more than others, and, should this be the normal expectation of every Christian? There are no sharply defined answers to so many of the questions we ask but what we can do is, firstly, learn as much as we can from those who have entered into this close relationship with God, and secondly, see how it may be confirmed through the Holy Scriptures.

After thirty or more years of studying the Bible and the teachings of the Church I have come to appreciate now what I believe is the quintessence of divine truth. It is this: that God who is love and loves all people, irrespective of place and time, has purposed to draw them into the closest possible love relationship with Himself. This He has purposed to do through the mediation of His only Son who made it possible through His sacrifice, death and resurrection.

No other Good News.

This is the only Good News that I can find in the Bible. It has nothing to do with being an evangelical, an anglican or a catholic. The Bible is about who God is, what He is doing and why. All other truths are incidental to this main truth. Think about this! Wasn't this the experience of St John of the Cross? The love of God drew him to the place of crucifixion where he died to self only to live to Christ and know a fresh intensity of this same love taking him ever onwards to a firmer union with the Father of all.

Let us see how we can relate this main truth to ourselves. To do this it might be helpful if we consider three statements: God loves all people, God draws people to Himself, and, He draws them through his Son's death and resurrection.

Will you please read each statement very carefully applying each new truth to yourself?

1. God loves ALL people.
The Scriptures, such as John 3:16, Romans 5:8, Ephesians 2:4–5 and 1 John 4:9–10 make this abundantly clear. We may reason as follows:

> 1. God has no favourites. His message of love is to all no matter to what race or colour or creed they may belong. God does not see people as Muslim, Hindu or

Tamil etc, but as those for whom He has a great love and to whom He is able to give abundant life if they will come to Him.

2. God cannot love any one more or less than He does. God loves! Not only does He love, but He *is* love (1 John 4:8).

3. This love is immeasurable, as immeasurable as God Himself. There are no degrees or variables. In a sense, God is life clothed and filled with love – and still a person.

4. However, the personal knowledge or experience of this love can only be truly appreciated if and as we receive it. This is an act of will on our part. The personhood of God may then be perceived.

2. *God draws people to Himself.*

The Bible is filled with the stories of God drawing attention to Himself. There are so many ways in which He made his intentions known to people living on this earth. (Examples are: Abraham, Moses, Samuel, King David, Peter, James, John the Divine, Paul). Some of the ways and means He used are quite astonishing. For example, read in Matthew 17 of Peter, James and John with Jesus on the Mount of Transfiguration. There were occasions when God spoke to people who were neither of Israel or the Church – Balaam and Nebuchednezzar. I think that we can safely record these observations.

1. God reveals Himself to anyone he chooses.

2. No revelation is without a specific purpose for this would be inconsistent with His nature.

3. God, who loves all people, is drawing people to Himself daily – through the natural things He has made – Romans 1:19–20.

4. The more common way in which Christians know this drawing power is through the agency of the Holy Spirit – John 14:17, 25–26, 15:25–27, 16:7–11.

5. The nature of God may be seen on each occasion.

6. Through them He makes clear His intentions, commandments, directions, judgements; He comforts, encourages, clarifies and edifies.

7. It is not necessarily an indication of a person's state of holiness. Any revelation to bring us closer to Himself is a gift through the mercy of God.

8. And every revelation is bound up in some inexplicable way with the redemptive plan and purposes of God. God really loves us and this world in which we live, and He wants it thoroughly changed for good. He is saying, 'Look at me, I want to speak of my love and of what I've done for you.'

3. He draws people through His Son's sacrifice.

There are so many scriptures in the New Testament relating to this subject; it is the principal theme. Matthew 20:28, 26:28, John 1:29, 12:24, 14:19, Acts 26:23, Romans 5:6–11, 6:3–5, 6:9–10, 8:3,32,34,39, Galatians 4:4–5 are but a very few.

However, I think that Ephesians 1:3–14 is the most profoundly informative of scriptures. There St Paul writes that God has blessed us with every spiritual blessing (v.3), that we have been chosen before the world was made (v.4), to be His sons (v.5), that we are redeemed through Christ's blood in order to be forgiven. Grace has been lavished on us (v.7), and he has revealed to us His will to unite all things in Him in heaven and on earth (vv.9,10). We have been appointed to live for the praise of His glory (v.12), and that He has guaranteed all this by sealing us with the promised Holy Spirit (vv. 13,14).

So these are our observations.

1. God's invitation is to all – including you and me.
2. His great love for us draws us to Himself, but only by the way of Christ's death and resurrection.
3. As we draw near we are made aware of our sinful

condition. Needless to say, this may be painful for we see ourselves as we really are.

4. But help is at hand for His forgiveness is as free as His invitation to come.

5. Forgiveness is another word for freedom. It also means an entrance into a closer union with God.

6. The life we live after such an encounter is what the Bible calls resurrection life.

All may draw near.

As I encouraged you earlier on please read through these observations, or stages of a journey if you wish, and ask yourself: what is your response?

I do want to make this point clear. What I have written is for the Christian as well as the person who would like to walk the Christian pathway. For the Christian it should mean a deeper understanding and union with God while for the earnest inquirer it could well mean the beginning of the journey towards God. Of one thing you may be sure, you will have no cause to regret your actions.

Now let us see if we can discover some practical ways of making use of what we have learned. Perhaps, as a Christian you have, for years, longed to know God much better than you do. You have heard your friends talking of their special times of prayer, of the guidance they have received and even how God has spoken to them. You have remained the silent listener fervently praying, 'Dear God, where are you in my life?' Do not give up! Remember, God has no favourites; his heart is open at all times and right now he welcomes you!

Stage One – drawing near.

How do we begin? Well, one of the facts that we must keep in mind is that although there is a part we have to play, it is God himself who will be drawing us – we must be willing to be drawn. Are we willing, I mean, really willing? Let us make this step one of the first stage.

1. *Willingness.*

In real life there are many times when we know we should obey God but we are far from willing. What do we do then? Well, God knows what we are able to do and what we are not, and He is always ready to encourage us at such times. I once heard a speaker say something like this and I think it is worth remembering.

'Lord, at this time I feel so unwilling. Please help me to be willing to be made willing. Amen.'

I have prayed that same prayer many times – and it has worked.

2. *Trust.*

Proverbs 3:5 says, 'Trust in the Lord with all your heart and do not rely on your own insight.'

It takes time and understanding to learn how to trust a person. If you are beginning to learn how to trust God, tell Him so. Always be as honest as you can when talking to Him. It is not that He does not know the truth about you, rather, it helps you to know about yourself. There will be more about learning how to trust God later on in this book, but for now, we will keep in mind that our goal is to trust Him with the whole heart.

Whenever we do trust God the mind is apt to cause certain doubts to rise within us. We try to reason around whatever has been promised, and in so doing, we may weaken this trust. God may tell us one thing and our minds tell us another. Now because our knowledge is the result of an accumulation of a lifetime of experiences and has shaped us accordingly, we tend to give way to what we term common sense. Perhaps a prayer like this will be helpful.

Lord, I really want to learn how to trust you but I

need your help. Help me keep my mind from coming into conflict with whatever you are showing me or asking me to do.

3. *Commitment.*

Being committed to God is an act of will on our part and it really means being given to God. We have to ask ourselves whether we can trust ourselves to Him, whether we are willing to do whatever He desires. Do you think this is asking too much? If you do, then consider it this way. If this is the God who created us as well as the heavens and the earth, if this is He who has ordered all things so perfectly for millions of years, then who greater can we trust?

In chapter four of the Epistle of James we are provided with some very helpful advice. James is explaining to Christians who were finding the Christian path difficult to walk how, through obedience and renewed commitment, God could enter more fully into their lives. He says, 'God yearns jealously over the spirit which he made to dwell in us . . . and he gives grace to the humble (vv.5–6). Draw near to God and he will draw near to you (v.8). Humble yourselves before the Lord and he will exalt you' (v.10).

I see this as another way of saying that God's life is tied up with ours, and that if we are willing, He will give to us all the grace we need to do whatever He asks. If we will give Him our full attention – if we will draw near to Him – if we will be conscious of our needs and weaknesses, then He will be able to lift us up and bring us close to himself.

To summarise this first stage, we see our willingness to be drawn to God, our trust and our commitment to Him, as the preparation of ourselves for the second stage of the experience. But, please, may I add this. Each of these steps is interrelated with the other two, and because God treats us very much as individuals, each of us may expect variations and degrees of interior experience. This is not an efficiency test, rather, look upon it as a beautiful learning process to help us love Him more.

Stage Two – Understanding.

Our understanding of anything at all will depend in part on what we know about it. We are talking here about knowledge we receive through the senses – knowledge about everyday things. However, there is a knowledge we receive from spiritual sources but this can be received only by our spirits, or if you wish, the spiritual part of us. We can do little to hasten this except to prepare ourselves to receive it. Some part of this spiritual knowledge may be communicated to the mind, and when it is we usually find great difficulty in sharing it with others. This seems to be the major problem experienced by the mystics. There were not enough words in the human languages of the world to express with any adequacy their interior experience. It means that if we desire to understand their experience then we shall need the help of the one who inspired them – God.

These simple principles apply to us too. Briefly, they are these.

1. Let us give ourselves to reading and appreciating the Scriptures concerning the work of Jesus Christ – especially His life, death, and resurrection as described in the New Testament. Try to gain a more comprehensive view of what happened. Theological skills are not necessary.

2. Meditate on this knowledge. Don't be afraid of asking questions of it. Be in an attitude of prayer yet be as relaxed as possible; enjoy this time. You may think about various issues through the day when you are not too busy. Always keep before you the main objective which is that you might develop a deeper relationship with God.

3. Be expectant, but only for what God chooses to reveal to you. Very few people have experiences like St

John of the Cross but all may receive understanding, both mental and spiritual, for He desires all of us to be drawn to Him.

Stage Three – Receiving.

1. Different forms of revelation.

God uses no single form of revelation to show us what His Son has done on our behalf, but when He does, it is with infinite care for who we are – human beings. The varieties of ways He has used to speak to people in the past lead us to believe that His concern is never to frighten us, or to make us objects of scorn – never! But having said this, when it suits His purposes, this variety of ways may embrace a whole range of experiences from the still small voice to dramatic imagery.

Usually, receiving understanding is a progressive experience. It is as if each stage is a preparation for the next. Little by little God unfolds the mystery of His great redemptive plan and always the central truth is the Cross with Jesus Christ as its principal character. Through the study of His word and obedience to it, He is able to make the events of nearly two thousand years ago vividly alive and applicable to our present needs. He speaks through our minds and our spirits so that there are occasions when we may be able to share with others what we receive and occasions when words are totally inadequate.

2. Revelation with impact.

When God chooses to make a greater impact or impress a particular aspect of truth He may employ a vision, a dream, or a mental image. This does not mean that we have no more to receive or learn, far from it, rather, it makes us ask many more questions and seek better understanding of the things we know. Visions, dreams and mental impressions are given by the will of God and should not be sought after. One thing I have noticed is that they occur more often at times of crisis, when there is an urgent need for direction or comfort.

Canon David McInnes, a missioner of the diocese of Birmingham, experienced such a vision which helped him to become conscious of what the victory of the Cross meant. He said that he knew the theology of Christ as victor but did not know the reality: he lacked confidence and authority. He tells what he saw in his own words.

'I found myself crouching behind what seemed to be a post of a fence. Beyond the post there was a massive accumulation of armoured vehicles formed in such a way as if preparing to advance. These vehicles began to rev up, the noise was overwhelming and deafening. Then, as if bidden by some unseen leader, they began to move towards me. As I looked at the post in front of me it seemed to stretch up higher and hanging on it was the body of Christ. I knew that the armoured vehicles were directed towards me personally and as they hurled themselves at me, I was well aware that Christ's body was hanging there and that He would catch the full impact. Suddenly, there was the noise of a terrible impact – and then, silence. The breathing had stopped.'

Could any revelation be more graphic? David McInnes is one of God's gracious diplomats, a man who walks very close to Jesus.

An invitation.

If I could write another beatitude I think it would be something like this. 'Blessed are those who make themselves available to the Cross of Christ and His love for they shall know true holiness, and by it, they shall see God.'

We need not be afraid. Our sins will not overcome us; we shall not be turned away, for the Cross is the way to our Father's heart. And so, begin by being willing. Do not be in a hurry or press the Lord for some particular revelation; being drawn to Him is a gentle process.

Remember to read the Scriptures; delight in them and ask God to help you to understand them. Wait patiently before Him and the light of understanding which your heart desires will grow a little brighter every day.

Here is a prayer to help you begin.

Holy Father, Lord of love and revelation, you have told me that I am made in your image and likeness. I thank you for this promise. I know too that the way to your heart is through the crucified and resurrected Lord, Jesus Christ. Please help me to become willing to be drawn into His full embrace.

Change my believing into knowledge, my self-centredness into Christ-centredness, my unbelief into joyful certainty. As you reveal to me the true condition of my soul, make clear to me the grace of your forgiveness for this is the freeing power my life needs. Thank you, Lord, that when I confess my sins you are faithful and just to forgive me.

And, Holy Father, help me from this day to become more acquainted with your Holy Scriptures. Freely impart to my mind and spirit all truth with understanding so that my involvement with you through your Son will stimulate in me a true love response for you. I know that my walk of holiness depends on this. I humbly ask for your help and guidance in all things, through Jesus Christ, my Lord and God. Amen.

2: Emmanuel – God with us.

On my desk there is a small card on which there is an inscription by St Bernard. It reads, 'The measure of loving God is to love Him without measure.' This is what the Cross is all about. It is loving God and being loved by Him, or, being as close to Him as it is possible. Needless to say we shall never arrive at such a goal while here on earth, but we can follow the pathway. A brief review of our lives will show us that in spite of our many failures and setbacks, we are actually growing in the knowledge and experience of this love. However, if we want this love to be fragrance for our living, we must learn each day how to live and identify a little more closely with the suffering and glorified Christ. To help make this possible, I propose that we consider how Christ came from His Father in heaven and was born into the world to take the pathway to the Cross.

Perhaps the best place to start is to recognise that Christ was with God, and even was God, long before any form of creation existed (John 1:1–2). This is a truth our minds find difficult to grasp. Christ was a person within the context of the Godhead long before the angels and the archangels were created, even before heaven itself was brought into being. (We shall not discuss the nature of eternity here.) Then, at some time unstated in the great plan of God, the glorious heavenly host of angels, archangels, cherubim and seraphim were brought into existence. All the details are unknown to us now but, one day, such matters will be made clear. For the present we must content ourselves by gazing through the windows of the sacred scriptures and seeing everything in part. At such times we invite the Holy Spirit to be our interpreter and guide.

A Son is born – in heaven.

Hebrews, chapter one, provides the clue to what seems to have happened next. It relates to the moment when a son – God's only Son – was born of God, which makes this same God Father.

'For to what angel did God ever say, "Thou art my Son, today I have begotten thee?" ' (verse 5.)

Now this was a remarkable revelation to the heavenly host for they had no idea of the father-son relationship. We who live on this earth understand, for it is only by being born that we become inhabitants of this earth. Can you imagine how the angels felt? It was something totally new to them. They knew that they were directly created by their Creator, but they knew little about Him. They certainly could not penetrate His nature to discover His innermost secrets. And now, there before them, stood this new angel who was not an angel. Their creator was telling them that it was His only Son He was presenting to them.

I have often wondered whether at that time God explained to that startled company what he had in mind concerning his plan for saving the world. I have wondered too whether the universe and mankind had yet been created. It does not really matter. What does matter is that we see this as the first revelation of the Anointed One – the Christ – coming from the Godhead and proceeding on a journey that would inevitably and unswervingly take Him to the dreadful sacrifice of the Cross.

Here we must consider the nature of His coming to earth.

A Redeemer – both God and man.

The mystery of the Godhead is something we shall never fathom, but of this we can be sure, God created the universe and everything it contains, and He did it through his only Son, Jesus Christ (Gen. 1:1, cf John 1:3). Why? Well, firstly, because it pleased him to make it (Rev. 4:11), secondly, because he determined that it should be the stage on which man would dwell. And because He loved man so much (John 3:16), there He would redeem him from his fallen condition (John 1:11).

But what made Christ so special? Was it because He was God and therefore a super-power? Not at all. Christ could do nothing at all about man's plight if He remained in heaven, and He could nothing except sympathise if He came to earth as God. What mankind needed more than anything else was some person who understood the case for God's righteousness and abhorrence for sin, yet at the same time, was able to identify in every possible way with man in his lost condition. Not only this, he had to be able to do something about it. To put it another way, this special person needed to have the same motive as God for saving man from his lost condition, in fact, He had to be God. Then it was necessary for Him to be made a man with no special privileges at all, to make it possible for mankind to identify with Him and be reconciled back to God. As I have said, the only person who could do that was God's own Son, who was God.

Such a person is called a redeemer and a reconciler. 2 Corinthians 5:19 says, that in Christ, God was reconciling the world to Himself, not counting their trespasses against them.

Jesus Christ – perfect God.

There are many Scriptures that make it clear that Christ is God (Matt. 1:23, John 1:1, Rom. 9:5, Titus 2:13, 1 John 5:20 for example), but none so much as the beautiful statement in Colossians 1:15–20. These words describe with such simplicity and majesty His origin, His work of creation, His divine intention to redeem mankind through the Cross, reconciling all things back to Himself. Never in a thousand years could the mightiest angel being or the holiest person accomplish such a work.

> For this cause Christ did not count equality with God a thing to be grasped, but emptied Himself, taking the form of a servant, and was born in the likeness of men
>
> (Phil. 2:6–7).

Surrendered to the Cross.

Jesus Christ as God poses a question. How was His entrance into the world unique in terms of His human nature? Well, if God in Christ became a perfect man, then He must have accepted not only the limitations and influences imposed by the physical universe but also the existing conflicts and struggles of human relationships. We begin to understand the meaning of full surrender. Remember, He was without sin. It is impossible to liken it to any human experience. Perhaps the nearest we can get is to liken it to someone who has lived his life in a state of near perfect happiness, surrendering all his possessions and close associations with his loved ones, and entering one of the worst concentration camps known to man. Why the dramatic contrast? Because He who knew no sin, who had known only the most intimate relationship with His Father, had surrendered Himself to a completely hostile environment with no possibility of return apart from the way of the Cross. Here He was on earth, so pure and sinless, and except for His mother, there was not a person He could truly share His soul with.

Awareness of His divine mission.

This leads us to another question. How soon did He become aware of His divine mission? No doubt it was a gradual awareness but it must have been quite early in His life. The reasons I offer are these.

We simply do not know whether we have some kind of pre-existent life but we do know that Christ did. He must have been fully alive to who He was right up to the moment He left his heavenly splendour. At Mary's conception, through the intervention of the Holy Spirit (Luke 1:35), He became a human soul but His spirit had to be the Spirit of God. This was how God was to work out his redemptive plan through His Son Jesus. Unfortunately, we know very little about the nature of the spirit of man but it is quite certain that our fallen condition does not lend itself to free communication with God. With Jesus it had to be different. There were no obstructions, no genetical impairment, the Spirit of God was alive in all His fullness in Jesus from the moment He was conceived. It is my belief that He grew as nature intended Him to grow, but having a mind and spirit that developed with all possible God-awareness, He rapidly grew in the knowledge and understanding of His divine mission.

About the Father's business.

At the age of twelve years we find Him in the temple at Jerusalem sitting among the teachers listening to them and asking them questions. It says in Luke 2:47 that all who heard Him were amazed at His understanding and His questions. When Joseph and Mary, who had been searching for Him, finally found Him, they wanted to know why He had caused them so much anxiety. Jesus replied, 'How is it that you sought me? Did you not know that I must be in my Father's house?' (verse 49).

It is quite evident that Jesus at the age of twelve years

was versed in matters which had taken the teachers years to learn. These are the first recorded words of Jesus. It has been said that they are a prophecy of that consciousness of direct Sonship, closer and more ineffable than that of any other of the sons of men, which is afterwards the dominant idea of which His whole life is a manifestation.

I have laid emphasis on these truths for a good reason. If we can spend time getting to grips with the substance of them, then the more we will marvel at the nature of Christ's sacrifice on our behalf. Too often, when we consider the tortured frame of Jesus hanging on the Cross, we see the man and not too much of God. But if we can understand something more of the depth of meaning of the Incarnation, then we shall see the Father's eyes filled with profound love gazing at us through the agonised eyes of His beloved Son.

A personal faith and imagination exercise.

This kind of exercise can benefit you considerably. We are using our minds to think about holy things. Our faith is in the integrity of the Holy Scriptures and in the promise that the Holy Spirit will bring to our remembrance all the things He has taught us (John 14:26). And so, choose a time and place where you can be alone. Make sure you are comfortable and have your Bible with you. On the first and second occasions you may find the thoughts of the day crowding in on you. Don't give up. The more you practise this spiritual exercise the more relaxed and proficient you will become.

The passage to read is Matthew 2:8–20. Read it three or four times, the last time read it very carefully so that the events are painted on your mind. Allow the story to unfold with yourself as an observer or one of the characters.

The angel's announcement to the shepherds.

Here is an example of what I mean. You are with the shepherds who are watching over the sheep by night. These are special sheep and are being reared for burnt offerings and thank offerings for the temple at Jerusalem. The night is cold and the stars are shining brightly in the sky. As watchful as ever, you and the shepherds gather your garments closer around you and move a little nearer to the fire. You notice how they gaze every now and then into the darkness, discerning any unusual sound or movement. To all outward appearances the night seems uneventful but the sheep appear restless, not frightened, rather, expectant. They move together, their heads turned upwards as if waiting for someone.

Now what's this? Something's happening – there is a bright light in the sky and as you look at it it grows wider and brighter. Is there no limit to the brightness? As you gaze in sheer wonder you realise that the light is that of an angel. This is the glory of the Lord, and all around you now it shines like the sun in full strength. The shepherds are terrified, so are you, but the voice of the angel is heard, 'Don't be afraid for I am bringing you good news of a great joy which will come to all the people, for to you is born this day in the city of David a Saviour, who is Christ the Lord.' You hear the instructions how to find him. But such is the announcement that you are compelled to continue looking upwards, and as you do, the sky appears to erupt into a host of angel beings who shout their praises to God, 'Glory to God in the highest, and on earth peace among men with whom he is pleased.'

You find the manger.

You are running now with the shepherds to the place where this Christ has been born. In your mind you are puzzling how God's Son can be born in a common manger. In your dishevelled state you ask any person you meet where He is; you are sure that the whole world has heard the announcement. But they shake their heads and wonder at your madness. You run on.

And then you find the place. It *is* a manger; the angel was right. You are standing outside the stable and you can see it by the dim light of a flickering lamp. You stand still looking at each other as if waiting for a signal to move forward. You feel a constraining force drawing you to the manger side. You know you are on holy ground. You feel wanted; Joseph and Mary smile their welcome. The poverty and smells fade for this is the royal Son's chamber. Your legs are trembling and you want to kneel, the shepherds are kneeling too.

And there He is.

This is God's only Son. This is the sovereign Lord of glory. This is the creator of the heavens and earth. This is love made flesh – this tiny babe.

Come and worship.

Now spend as much time as you can just gazing upon Him. Think, this is your God – perfect God and perfect man. This is He who has come from the realms of glory. This is He before whom angels and archangels bow and offer their homage. This is your God demonstrating His everlasting love for you. This little mite is born to die for you.

Then, with thankful heart worship him. Allow the Holy Spirit to interpret all that you see in your mind. You will return to your daily life strengthened and encouraged, and you will understand the meaning of the cross so much better.

Jesus Christ – perfect man.

From the time of his birth, Christ really assumed the title Jesus Christ, for Jesus means, 'For he shall save his people from their sins' (Matt. 1:21). Even before He was presented to the angel host in the heavenly places, he was the Christ – the Anointed One, appointed to become the saviour of His people. We may reasonably assume this. Whether Hee was ever referred to there as Jesus, we do not know, but from the time of the Annunciation the Gospels make a great deal of this title because the writers are concerned with the record of Godd mediating through a man – the Christ on earth.

The Gospels demonstrate the truth that at no time did Jesus enjoy special privileges or advantages. He was born of a woman, in a stable, partaking of flesh and blood. He was circumcised as was the Jewish custom, and lived as other young people of his time. We read of him weeping at the tomb of Lazarus (John 11:35), of being hungry after his long forty-day fast (Matt. 4:2), of His thirst when He met the Samaritan woman at Jacob's well (John 4:7), of sleeping in the storm-tossed boat on the Galilean Sea. He could become weary (John 4:6), and be deeply moved (John 11:33), and above all, He knew what it was to suffer. When His time had come to be delivered up, His captors mocked and beat Him (Luke 22:63–65). Herod with his soldiers listened to the chief priests and scribes vehemently and falsely accuse Him (Luke 23:10–11), and later, after being cruelly scourged (Matt. 27:26), He was nailed to a cross (Luke 23:33).

All this shows that, without doubt, He was a real man – a genuine human being. However, He was a genuine human being with a difference. While He could work on earth only within the terms of His humanity, being God too, meant that He understood suffering as no other human being could. Allow me to explain for appreciating this truth can bring much consolation and hope to those who are suffering.

Our suffering companion.

The difference between Jesus and all other men is that He never sinned. He was holy, blameless, unstained, and separated from sinners (Heb. 7:26), and yet he identified in every way with fallen man. Just consider what this means. It means that we may experience rejection, being despised, hated, ridiculed, slandered, and so on, and He can say to us, 'I know precisely what you're going through.' We may suffer deprivation, loneliness, attacks of the enemy, friendlessness, even abandonment, and He can say, 'I'm with you all the way, you're not alone.'

As fallen creatures we may suffer considerably, but can you imagine the degree of suffering Jesus experienced – because He was sinless? Our fallen natures create within us a certain immunity to these invasions. For example, if someone speaks badly and slanders us, we may be hurt, but isn't it true that quite often a spirit of retaliation rises within us and we may say, perhaps to no one in particular, 'I don't care a jot what he says!' So we try to brush it aside thus alleviating the pain. Christ could never do this; He suffered the blast of every attack made on Him. It is for this reason that Hebrews 4:15 can mean so much to us, especially when we suffer. It says, 'We have not a high priest who is unable to sympathise with our weaknesses, but one who in every respect has been tempted as we are, yet without sin.' It continues by inviting us to come to His throne of grace where we may receive comfort.

He invites us to come to Him.

Are you conscious of suffering at this moment? Have you been misunderstood, badly treated, belittled, rejected or uncared for? Or have you sinned in some particular way so that in your despair you feel certain there is no more hope for you? Or is your body racked with pain from some dreaded disease or sickness so that you are now at the place where you greatly fear tomorrow? Then for a few moments come and rest awhile. Gently turn your thoughts away from the suffering, the depression, or whatever has brought you low, and then fill your mind with the knowledge of His presence. He is near you now, so very near. Listen to Him saying to you something like this: 'I am the one who understands your pain more than any other, even more than you, my child. You see, I have entered into your suffering and I have conquered its power. Draw near to me and let me share this victory with you so that you never need feel alone again. Every temptation you experience, I too have experienced. Every grief, every sorrow, every pain, I have endured for your sake, for I became a man – a real man, and as a man I have become your substitute through what I have done. I have given my life that you might live. And so I invite you to come and sit at my feet and rest awhile. When you are rested put my yoke on your shoulders (for it is light), and learn what I will teach you. You will see that I am very gentle and quite unpretentious, and you will find rest for your soul.'

Jesus – Victim and Victor.

There are Christians who when they consider the Cross talk only of Jesus' victory, His mastery over the evil one and the release of the captives, perhaps finding it too painful to meditate overmuch on His sufferings. Others dwell with a certain morbidity on the pains He bore through the examinations, the scourgings and final crucifixion, almost to the exclusion of His victory, ascension and resurrection. They stand there in genuine sorrow and there they stay. Who knows the reason why? Perhaps it is a matter of temperament, or upbringing, or spiritual education, but of this we may be sure, we lose out somewhere along the line if we do not see the

Man of Sorrows and the Mighty King as one and the same Christ.

The meaning of the cross.

Like many others I have tried to visualise what happened when Christ died, and there is no doubt in my mind that the Cross is the place of crisis, the place of change. It is timeless. There He invites us to enter by faith into His death-destroying work and identify with Him in his sufferings and humiliation, that by the same token, we may receive His glorious life-giving freedom. The more we understand and appreciate His sufferings, the more wonderful His victory appears, for His sufferings and victory are all part of one work. God's life and the enemy, death, cannot co-exist! If I am in a state of sin then I cannot know the blessings of His life. Likewise, when I am enjoying the full measure His life, I cannot be in a state of sin.

Believing and receiving.

Believing and receiving always walk hand in hand. This is an important truth to remember whenever we come to Christ for forgiveness. In the past I used to obtain forgiveness of my sins in order that I might then ask for His life. This often ended in failure and unhappiness. It so happened that when I sinned I would approach the Lord for forgiveness after repentance, then I would wallow in a form of self-pity and wonder why there was no sense of peace and freedom. Oh yes, I believed that He would forgive me if I confessed my sins – the Bible said so – but usually I found it difficult to receive His vital new life until the sorrow from having sinned passed away. And what made matters worse, if I had little or no sense of sorrow then I believed there could be no forgiveness. I know that many Christians believe this. How wrong I was!

Much later, I was to learn that it was right to identify my sins and to confess them to the Lord, but the moment of my confession was the same moment I received His forgiveness. For me, it was when I was able to say, 'Thank you, Lord, I have asked believing and I have received.'

'Thank you,' or some similar expression is like a releasing agent. It is a form of declaration of the heart and mind that God longs for us to enjoy the fullness of His divine life, and therefore, the turning of the 'Thank you' key in the lock of truth is operated by faith. Remember, 'According to your faith be it done to you' (Matt. 9:29). We shall consider faith in another chapter.

One foot on the bottom.

To help us understand this truth a little better I will relate an incident from my teenage days. When I was about fourteen years of age I decided I would become a great swimmer. This arose from watching the town water polo team at work at the local baths. They were agile, strong, and fast in the water and I wanted to be like them. But all I did was to sit on the side of the baths and watch. I must confess that I lived in a dream world. I had a problem and no one knew what it was but myself. I could dive from the side, swim for a while under water, even swim from one side of the baths to the other. Well, that is what you would think if you watched me from a distance. What no one knew, however, was that I only swam the side stroke. And the reason? It was the only stroke that allowed me to swim with my big toe on the bottom. The last thing I wanted was for my friends to discover this.

Sink or swim.

What was my problem? Simply, it was this. Would the water support me if I committed myself to it? It did for millions of other people – I knew that – but would it for me?

One day, after a great mental struggle, I decided to

find out whether I could swim or not. It was literally sink or swim. And so, when the baths were reasonably empty, I casually made my way to the deep end and sat down on the top rung of the ladder. The moment of truth had come. Making every effort to appear nonchalant I climbed down into the water holding firmly to the rail in case I should slip. As I held myself away from it my body began to slide down into the water. Frantically, I pulled myself to the safety of the steps. My heart was pounding. What had gone wrong? Why did I sink? Then the truth filtered through my confusion and a measure of certainty was restored. Of course, I didn't swim! In a sense I had committed myself to sinking. I had to commit myself to floating and to swimming.

I pushed myself away from the rail once more and took a deep breath. Lying on my side I consciously surrendered myself to the water. I sank a little, but then, as I stretched out in the side stroke my body began to move through the water with an ease I had never experienced before. I was swimming! I was actually swimming!

Who can describe the moment when hope becomes reality; that transforming moment when 'cannot' becomes 'can', when walking by faith becomes walking by sight? And reverting to our 'Thank you' truth we see this as the verbal expression of intention transformed into positive action.

(By the way, I never became a great swimmer; it didn't seem to matter any more.)

Confession and feeling sorry.

Many Christians equate confession with feeling sorry. This cannot be done, there is an important difference. The Apostle John made it abundantly clear that if we confess our sins, and that means to acknowledge or to admit them, and are willing to turn from them (that is repentance), then Jesus will forgive us and cleanse us from all unrighteousness (1 John 1:9). Confession itself has nothing to do with feeling sorry, although we pray there will be accompanying sorrow when we confess. To be honest, there are occasions when the sense of having sinned and grieved God is almost absent. That can be worrying. Many a church teaches that sorrow is a prerequisite of forgiveness, but we may ask, how much sorrow is needed before forgiveness is granted by God? Do we have to remain in a state of sin until a certain level is reached? Thank God, this is not so! We are charged by St John to confess our sins, to state clearly what they are and to be willing to turn from them. It has been my experience that whenever I have done this, more often than not, genuine sorrow has been experienced for the sins I have committed, and with it, a great happiness for the forgiveness I have received. It is rather like God saying, 'Now live, for you are freed from your sins!' This is an important truth and we need to keep it in mind.

Yes, God is with us!

In the previous chapter we considered God drawing us ever closer to Himself through the work of His Son who triumphed over sin and death on the Cross. We saw that the Cross means death to self and life to the spirit, and that we are to embrace it. In this chapter we have seen how we are more able to do this through a deeper appreciation of Christ as perfect God and perfect man. Should we not be grateful for all that He has done for us? Can we deny Him the sole place in our hearts; is it not His by right? And yet He does not lay on us heavy and impossible demands, but He woos us to His side with such tenderness and compassion and He shelters us under the shadow of His wings.

Here is a prayer which may help you formulate your thoughts and feelings.

Holy Father, I think I'm beginning to understand something of the greatness of your Son, Jesus Christ. I want to draw nearer to you through Him but I need the enlightenment only you can give. Show me with the aid of your Holy Spirit the glorious mystery of the Incarnation – the birth and the life of my Saviour. Take me along this pathway to the Cross, where with fresh understanding, I may enter the embrace of those outstretched arms.

And gracious Father, help me to grasp with heart, mind, and spirit, the true meaning of forgiveness. Whatever you offer me, let me accept it, for I know that you will offer me nothing unless I need it. And all that you give, Lord, is given to bring me closer to you.

I humbly thank you for all you have done for this world in which I live. This is my desire, to share what I have received with others. Help me, Lord, through Jesus Christ my Saviour. Amen.

3: The Offer of Life

So far we have talked about Christ leaving the being of His Father and coming on His redemptive mission to earth, and how He was truly God and truly man. We saw that as perfect and sinless man He is able to identify with us in our sufferings, and that His earthly ministry was completed when He died on the Cross. We also assessed some of the great benefits we may enjoy by identifying with Him.

But what actually happened there? Why a cross? Why did He have to be nailed to it? How do we enter into His death and resurrection? These are important questions. While we may learn only some of the truth, what we learn can help us live out the meaning of the Cross in our daily lives.

The curse of the Law.

Have you ever tried keeping the ten commandments? Many have tried and failed. To put it mildly it is difficult, while to put it truthfully it's impossible. The standards are as high as God Himself. The ancient people of Israel couldn't keep them, and so God provided a special means to 'cover' their sins and this took place once every year on the Day of Atonement.

We are told that to accept the Law and not keep it in all its parts makes one accursed (Eph. 3:10), and that is a terrible business. Israel tried and failed miserably, and so will any man or woman no matter how good they may be.

Now, to be accursed means that one is cut off from the blessings of God. We cannot say to him, 'Look, Lord, I've tried so hard and I think I've succeeded in keeping nine tenths of it. Surely you can overlook the occasional failure or mistake.' It is not that He is not pleased that you have tried, if that is the limit of your knowledge of Him. It is rather that the one tenth we call failure He calls sin. That means, in plain words, that we are sinners, and a sinner cannot have communion with a holy God. However, what should encourage us is that this same God is a God of mercy and compassion. He has done something about the question of sin so that we may live and not die.

God's provision.

In Deuteronomy 21:22–23, we read of a strange provision in the Mosaic Law. If a man commits a crime punishable by death and his body is hanged on a tree, then his body must be taken down and buried before sunset. It says that a hanged man is accursed by God, and failure to carry out this operation will defile the land which is Israel's inheritance. Nowhere does it tell us why. However, St Paul makes reference to this Scripture in Galatians where he tells us how Christ became a curse for us by being hanged on a tree (or the Cross), and in so doing, redeemed us from the curse of the law (Gal. 3:13). Normally, a man who is hanged on a tree is one who has committed a crime, but Christ committed no crimes whatsoever; he was sinless. It is what the Church calls the doctrine of substitution, or, Christ dying for our sins, the righteous taking the place of the unrighteous (1 Peter 3:18).

You will notice that it does not say that He became a sinner, but it does say that He became sin for us. It also says in 1 Peter 2:24 that He bore our sins in His body on the tree (the Cross) that we might die to sin and live to righteousness. All I can say by way of explanation is that this is one of those doctrinal mysteries that we receive by faith. Nonetheless, if this is a mystery, be assured that the working out of the truth in our lives can be transforming.

The doorway to life.

Let us take a closer look and find out, if we can, what happened when our Saviour Christ was nailed to the Cross. I am a sincere believer that the Cross is the doorway to eternal life, which is the life of God. It is the place of radical change where death is destroyed and life is imparted, not only at the commencement of our Christian experience, but very much for our daily living.

Whenever sin engulfs us, whenever bad habits ensnare us, or the enemy assaults us, or when we are afflicted in mind, body or spirit, we have welcome access to the efficacy of Christ's work. He is ever ready to help in our time of need. He invites us to enter through this door even if our knowledge of what He has done for us is sparse. It is our willingness and earnest desire of the heart which matter to Him.

A shadow of good things to come.

John Kitto, in his *Cyclopaedia of Biblical Literature*, says of the word 'type', 'that the best definition in its theological sense is that which Hebrews 10:1 supplies, "a type is a shadow of good things to come", or as the apostle elsewhere expresses it (Col. 2:17), "a shadow of things to come".' He then points out some examples of types found in the Bible.

I think it reasonable to say that if you want to learn more about Christ and His plan for the ages to come then read carefully the Pentateuch (the first five books of the Bible). When Israel became a nation under God, she received from Him in great detail the terms of her relationship with Him. She was instructed how to conduct herself in her daily affairs, how to approach Him, how to remember His ever-presence and power, and what to do when things went wrong. The many different parts that went to make up this complex way of life can be said to be 'types', shadows of good things to come.

The high priest was a type of Christ ministering on behalf of the Church; the various sacrifices typifying the many aspects of His character, and that He was to become a victim and die sacrificially. It is the altar of burnt offering, God's appointed place of sacrifice, on which I will focus our attention. To better appreciate its significance, we must see it in the context of the tabernacle. This is the place where God met with His people, the place where His people ministered to Him.

The Tabernacle.

Imagine a large rectangle of ground, 75 x 150 feet, surrounded by a linen screen, supported by poles, with its axis east and west. This is the court of the tabernacle. If we pass through the gate at the eastern end, we will not fail to notice in the rear half of the courtyard a strangely constructed tent about 45 x 15 feet and 10 feet in height. This is the tabernacle.

The tabernacle is divided into two compartments with wooden sides overlaid with gold. Its roof comprises four coverings of linen, woollen materials, goats' hair and badgers' skins. The more westerly of the two compartments is called the Holy of Holies and it contains the ark of the covenant. Then, separated by an elaborate material partition, known as the veil, is the other compartment called the Holy Place. The Holy Place contains a seven-branched candlestick made of gold, a small altar in front of the veil for incense, and a table on which the priests place twelve loaves of special bread.

Outside, in front of the opening to the Holy Place, is a large brass bowl filled with water which the priests use for ceremonial washings. And it is between this brass bowl and the opening to the courtyard that we find the altar of burnt offering which we desire to learn more about.

This altar was made of shittim (or acacia) boards over-laid with brass sheets. It measured 8 feet x 8 feet, and was 5 feet in height, and had a large grid across the top on which the sacrifice was laid. It was probably filled with stones and earth. Around the lower part of the altar there was a ledge on which the priests could stand, and on the upper four corners there were brass horns to which the animal could be tethered.

The Altar Most Holy.

A few years ago I was reading part of the Book of Exodus when I made one of those delightful discoveries one makes every now and again.

I was fully aware that the sacrificial lamb was a type of Jesus Christ and that the altar must be a type of the Cross on which He died. But it was the details concerning the preparation that held my attention. Exodus 29:19–37 tells how Aaron and his sons were to be ordained as high priest and priests, and it was an elaborate ritual. Now along with the preparation and ordination of the priests was the preparation of the altar of burnt offering upon which they would lay their future sacrifices. Verses 36 and 37 describe how this was done.

> Also you shall offer a sin offering for the altar when you make atonement for it, and shall anoint it, to consecrate it. Seven days [the number of divine perfection] you shall make atonement for the altar and consecrate it . . .

All this made sense for the Lord desired all things relating to sacrifice and worship to be absolutely pure and given to Him, but notice what happened when on the seventh day the high priest for the last time sprinkled the blood and poured out the oil.

> . . . and the altar shall be MOST HOLY, and whatever touches the altar shall become HOLY.

What a remarkable statement! What was the meaning? How could holiness be transmitted by way of a touch? The altar was only a hollow wooden box covered with brass plates and of little value at today's prices. But of course, here we are dealing with eternal values. Next to the ark of the covenant in the Holy of Holies the altar of burnt offering was the most priceless possession to the Israelites. And the reason? Because the Lord God Almighty had declared it to be most holy. By its means His people could have continuous access to His throne by way of the appointed sacrifices and priesthood.

Our access is through the high priesthood and sacrifice of Christ.

Attempts to frustrate God's plan.

How shall we understand all this in the light of what Christ has done for us? How did He become the fulfilment of these types given to Israel so many years before He came to earth? What actually happened when He was nailed to the Cross? Once again I have to say that we can only understand in part but what part we may understand can be like the reviving wind in a hot desert.

We know that from the time Jesus was born into this world attempts were made by Satan and his hierarchy to frustrate God's plan for redeeming mankind. Satan was fully aware that the only person who could accomplish this mission was God's Son, Jesus Christ. The success of the mission depended on three factors. The first was that Christ should never sin in any way. The second was that He should reach his destination, the Cross, where He must die a sacrificial death, and the third was, that when He was offered, He would be a perfect and an acceptable offering according to the Mosaic Law. He was the antitype of the Passover lamb which had to be offered without spot or blemish (1 Peter 1:19). And so, for Satan to frustrate God's plan he had to cause Jesus to sin, making Him an unacceptable offering, or arrange His premature death.

. . . but all attempts failed.

All the attempts he made on Jesus failed. The first was to murder Jesus when He was but a child. This was at Herod's instigation when he ordered a massacre of infants after he had heard from the wise men that they were looking for a child who was purported to be the king of the Jews (Matt.2:16). Clearly, he was a tool, and Satan used his craving for power for his own ends.

The second attempt took the form of temptation. After a forty-day fast Satan came to Jesus in His weakened state and tempted Him through the lust of the flesh, the pride of life and the lust of the eye. After Jesus had countered this enemy by using the Holy Scriptures Satan was commanded to leave Him (Matt.4:1–11). He failed utterly to make Jesus sin.

If we look carefully at the Scriptures we shall see other attempts when the Jews were incited by their leaders to bring about His premature death. But it is the final attempt which attracts our attention most. If Satan failed on this occasion he knew there would be no hope at all for him. We are talking about Christ's death on the Cross.

Satan – the father of lies.

What I have to say now is my own assessment and impression of what I think happened. I will attempt to interpret the types we discussed earlier on in the light of their fulfilment. See what you think.

Satan (often called the devil), from the time he fell from God's grace, did his utmost to defeat God's redemptive plan by employing every form of cunning and deceit. Concerning his integrity, John 8:44b says that he was a murderer from the beginning and has nothing to do with the truth because there is no truth in him. When he lies he speaks according to his own nature for he is a liar and the father of lies. What a terrible indictment. Now a lie, when it is told enough times, can be believed to be the truth. This, I feel, was Satan's mistake. He believed that if he could mobilise all the forces at his command so that Jesus could be nailed to a cross (or a tree), then the offering would be null and void in God's sight. What seems so strange is that he was able to believe this in spite of the fact that he knew that God had destined His Son to die this way. But then, if he is the father of lies, why should he not believe his own lie?

The confidence of God.

When the time had come, Jesus was taken to the place of his execution. The dreadful task of nailing Him to the wooden cross fell to the Roman levies. They had no idea of what they were doing other than they were putting another poor wretch to death; it was a commonplace duty. But in the unseen realms two great powers watched and waited. The believer in his lie waited for the near moment when evil would triumph over good, and the hope of countless millions would be snatched from them and trodden under foot for ever, and the Lord of all truth and compassion waited, knowing that, very soon, His only Son would destroy the power of sin and death, once and for all time, and return home to Him. All this was planned from the beginning and must take place.

And this is what happened.

The perfect sacrifice.

As they threw Jesus down and pinned His hands and feet with cruel spikes to the cross, so the blood flowed freely soaking into the wood of the cross. In that moment He became accursed just as it tells us in the Book of Deuteronomy. This was what St Paul is talking about in Galatians 3:13 where he says that Christ redeemed us from the curse of the law, having become a curse for us – for it is written, 'Cursed be everyone who hangs on a tree.' But the truly remarkable thing about Jesus being cursed instead of us is the manner in which He dealt with it.

You will remember, earlier on, we saw that the altar of burnt offering received the sacrifices prescribed by the Law, and this finds its fulfilment in the cross receiving the sacrifice of Jesus Himself. You will remember too that the altar of burnt offering could accept no offerings until it had been atoned for with blood and consecrated with oil. What about the cross – the altar on which Christ was offered up?

The answer is that the cross was atoned for with the shed blood of Christ, and consecrated through His given life, which is in the blood (Lev. 17:11). Oil is a symbol of God's life – the Holy Spirit. So we see the seven-fold (or perfect) atonement and consecration of the altar of burnt offering fulfilled in Christ offering a perfect atonement and consecration for the cross with his own lifeblood.

And the result?

As Jesus was nailed to His cross He became accursed for us, but the outpouring of the blood onto the cross destroyed this accursed condition because it was a perfect atonement and a perfect consecration for the cross. In this way it became the MOST HOLY place on earth.

Both events took place at the same time.

What it means to us today.

When we approach the Cross today for forgiveness this two-fold principle is operative in our lives. Firstly, our sins are forgiven, and secondly, in the same moment of time, we are declared HOLY, or to put it another way, we are given His life. We are not left hanging between being forgiven and receiving His life. The receiving of His forgiveness and being made holy is the 'touching' of the Cross. For practical purposes we may interpret this as the act of saying, 'thank you,' or, 'Lord, I receive your forgiveness and your life.'

Whenever I meditate on this truth, although I know He is risen and is sitting on the Father's right hand, I still see the Cross as God's meeting place with men and women. It is the most holy place where the Saviour stands with one hand reaching up to His beloved Father and the other hand outstretched to us. He is the perfect mediator and interpreter of our cries. When I come to Him with my sins, my problems, my brokenness, I take that hand of His and I seem to hear Him say, 'Father, here is one of your children in need. Accept him for my sake so that he may know that we are one.' My act of touching the Cross is through my prayer, 'Lord, I believe.'

St Catherine of Siena, the great fourteenth-century saintly teacher, saw Jesus as a bridge. She says in the only book she ever wrote, *The Dialogue*, 'I want you to look at the bridge that is my only begotten Son, and notice its greatness. Look! It stretches from heaven to earth, joining the earth of your humanity with the grandeur of the Godhead. This is what I mean when I say it stretches from heaven to earth – and constitutes the union that I have made with man.' She closes the chapter by adding, 'But my Son's having made of himself a bridge for you will not bring you to life unless you use it.'

Can we resist this invitation from the heart of God the

Father, to be drawn near, and so, to stay near. If we cannot trust Him, who then can we trust? The bridge is ready to be used, His arms are open wide.

Hand in hand – forgiveness and life.

From all that we have been discussing there are two observations we may make regarding Christ's ministry, not only now, but also when He walked this earth.

Firstly, whenever He ministers to people He identifies with them. He enters into their sufferings and broken condition without being overpowered by them. He remains pure and unstained. The willingness and desire to be free from sin and sickness is the act of faith necessary for Him to release to them His divine life and forgiveness.

Secondly, and this is an extension of the first and is based on Scriptural evidence, when He had finished preaching, His ministry always took the forms of forgiveness of sins and healing – mind, body and spirit. I will explain what I mean.

Forgiveness is the freeing from the bondage of sin, and sin is a destructive and death-dealing force. We cannot measure it, and we know so little about its nature, but there is enough evidence of the havoc it causes in our lives. Unfortunately, other people can be the victims of our sinful deeds. On the other side of the forgiveness coin is healing, which is the bringing together into a natural unity all those parts that have been separated or damaged by sin. By this, I am not implying that if you are still sick after repentance and forgiveness there must be some hidden sin you have not confessed. There are a number of reasons that we cannot go into now. What we do see from Christ's ministry is that forgiveness was always associated with the imparting of life. Let us consider the incident in Matthew 8:1–4 when the leper was healed.

The healing of the leper.

We read that a leper broke his imposed bounds and hurried with all speed through the horrified crowds to Jesus who had just entered the town. There before Him he knelt while the watching religious leaders saw this as an opportunity not to be missed. Any one knew that a true master in Israel would immediately turn from a leper, but this man . . . why, He actually talked to him.

'Lord, if it is your will, you can make me clean,' said the leper. Now notice, Jesus did two things. He said, 'I will, be thou clean,' while at the same time He did the unpardonable thing. He deliberately reached out his hand and touched the leper who, the account tells us, was immediately made clean.

I can well imagine a conversation something like this between the religious leaders and Jesus.

'Look, everybody! This man, Jesus, who claims to be a rabbi and a teacher, has just broken the Law before your very eyes. Now what has he to say for himself?'

'But how have I broken the Law,' looking at them serenely.

'How? Isn't it evident to any godly Israelite? You've become ceremonially unclean!'

'And how did that happen?'

'Are you so slow-witted? You actually touched a leper!' Can you see Jesus looking around at the people who are silent and waiting, then at the cleansed man who is grinning from ear to ear, and back to the leaders who are now feeling a little uncomfortable? Can you see the slight smile playing on his lips as he says to them,

'What leper?'

The cry from the heart.

This is a beautiful example of Jesus identifying with a broken man and healing him (and I believe forgiving him too) through the imparting of His life.

Notice that the leper did not say, 'Lord, forgive me my sins, and then, will you cleanse me of my leprosy?' No, he said, 'Lord, if you will you can make me clean.' Jesus did not reprove him but reached out his hand and touched him.

Not for a moment am I saying that we need not acknowledge and confess our sins. Rather, it is that coming into the presence of a holy God in a sinful condition cannot leave us unmoved and unresponsive. I have often found that long before my prayer of repentance has reached my lips in the formal manner, my soul has uttered it, and I am quite sure that it has been heard by God. Don't you think this is true? This must have happened many times to people who came to Jesus when He walked this earth. They knew they were forgiven as they received His life, or, to put it another way, the life they received became the declaration that they had been forgiven. His life is like a releasing agent.

Which is easier?

Do you remember the paralytic who was lowered through the roof by his friends because of the crowds who filled the doorway? Well, it says in Mark 2:5, that when Jesus saw their faith, He said to the man, 'My son, your sins are forgiven.' But he hadn't asked for his sins to be forgiven, although I am convinced that he knew he was a sinner, especially when he found himself in the presence of the holy Christ.

When the scribes who were present began to question Jesus' authority, He said to them, 'Why do you question thus in your hearts? Which is easier, to say to the paralytic, "Your sins are forgiven", or to say, "Rise, take up your bed and walk." ' (Mark 2:8–9).

I can only conclude that the imparting of His life to heal may also include the forgiveness of sins. As we give ourselves to Christ, that is, to the very best of our ability, so He gives Himself to us, forgiving us, when necessary, and giving to us His abundant life which is true freedom.

Healed from arthritis through forgiveness.

To present this truth in a twentieth-century context may I share with you an incident from the life of the Reverend Reginald East, one of the founders of the Barnabas Fellowship in Dorset. I will attempt to relate the details as accurately as possible from his own words.

'I was in parish work and experiencing certain difficulties at the time. Things were not going well, certainly not as I wanted them to go, and I was growing very disheartened. In addition to this I was growing bitter with God and with my congregation. I was always getting at them and criticising them in my attempt to push them into a deeper life with God.

'One day, I discovered that I had arthritis in one of my fingers and this spread slowly through the rest of my body. I was in much pain and I felt very depressed. About this time God wonderfully baptised me with the Holy Spirit. The first thing he required of me was to ask his forgiveness, and then to ask the forgiveness of my congregation. On the following Sunday I stood before my people and shared with them the wrong I had done them. I had tried to use them instead of loving them. Now, would they forgive me?

'From that day the arthritis commenced to leave me through prayer until I was completely freed. I have had no trace of it since. That was twenty-five years ago.' I assure you that this is the testimony of a man of integrity who has served God with his wife, Lucia, for many years.

But what of you and me? Can God do the same for us? Certainly he can – if we will allow him. Nevertheless, the way may be through repentance, confession and forgiveness, but it's worth it.

Here is a prayer you may find helpful.

Gracious Father, I believe that Jesus Christ, your Son, has triumphed over sin and death. I believe that through His death and resurrection He has opened the way to eternal life. I believe, too, that the Cross has become the most holy place on earth. It is here where I am released from my sins and all forms of brokenness.

And so, with a humble and contrite heart, I come to you with my wounds, my pains, my failures, my weaknesses, and my sins. I confess and repent of all that makes me unclean, of all that hinders my communion with you. Forgive me, holy Lord, cleanse me into the way of your truth.

All glory and thanks I give to you. From this day I will try to serve you with a pure desire. Daily will I receive the release and freedom which you have obtained for me through your sacrifice. Accept this prayer, Holy Father, for I offer it in the Name of Jesus Christ who is forever Lord. Amen.

4: Growing into His likeness.

Discovering the deeper meaning of the Cross is rather like embarking on a voyage of discovery; there are unlimited opportunities ahead of us. No longer are we alone to fend for ourselves, no longer need we be friendless, and no longer will the pathway of life be difficult to find. The blessed Holy Spirit has become our friend; our constant companion, protector, guide and sustainer in all times of trouble. What more can a person want? We cannot fail, can we?

Of course, while all this is the truth in theory, the working out of it is a process that takes time. There are disciplines we have to learn to bring order to our lives, patience, so that we do not anticipate God, and often, courage to go on when we feel like giving up. Now that makes it appear like a lot of hard work, doesn't it? Well, what we shall see in this chapter is that hard work is not the answer but learning to be natural is. I learned this lesson the hard way and discovered too that I was not alone.

An honest appraisal.

I remember speaking at a conference at Canterbury some years ago, and to this gathering of many hundreds of people I presented some questions. I asked for truthful answers.

The first question was, 'Please raise your hand if you do not really enjoy your daily times of prayer and Bible study?' The response was of great hesitation at first, just a few hands here and there, but as I waited other hands began to rise, many hands, scores of hands; and some heads were bowed too.

I asked my second question. 'Will you please raise your hand if your experience as a Christian is too often one of failure?' Once again, many, many hands were raised.

And finally, my third question. 'Do you, even in the midst of friends and loved ones, experience abnormal rejection and loneliness for a Christian?' A similar number of hands were raised.

I will not forget that day in a hurry for I realised with sadness that this unhappy response was but a token expression of the malady from which most of the Church of Christ suffered. No, I am not saying that the Church has failed but it is suffering from a sort of spiritual anaemia. Of course, doubts and fears of many kinds are bound to confront us as we pass through this life; but it is the unreasonable doubts and fears that cling to us like barnacles on the bottom of a boat that I am concerned with. We say that God is moving by His Spirit, but why so much spiritual helplessness mingled with a good measure of guilt?

Keeping pace with the Spirit.

May I suggest an answer for you to consider? I feel sure that in this 'age of the Spirit', He is calling each member of His Church to give himself, not so much to great works and successful ventures of faith, but to being 'planted' wherever He wills, to a surrender of mind and will, and that growing is learning how to become whatever He wants us to be. Then, we shall grow at a rate comparable to what the Holy Spirit is doing. This is the right and natural way.

Let us stop blaming our leaders for their indifference or intolerance, or our neighbour for his lack of understanding and love, and look within ourselves to see if we are willing to accept our obligations to grow into the fullness and stature of our blessed Lord. There is no other way; but what does it mean in terms of practice? Before I share with you some important principles of growing, may I relate to you a personal experience? You may in some parts be able to identify with it for it makes clear what God does not want to happen to us.

Leaving home.

About a year after my mother died my father married for a second time and the lady of his choice was a retired grammar school headmistress. My brother, David, and I managed a reasonable relationship with her but there were moments when we were almost certain that she regarded us as two of her former pupils. We kept the peace for our father's sake.

One day, some months after the wedding, our father and stepmother made it clear that they would like us to leave home and find somewhere else to live. They said they required time together to work out their new relationship. Now, it seems a reasonable request, but then, so soon after our mother's death, we felt as if we were being turned out into the street. David found some digs near to his place of employment while I went to live with a friend who lived alone on a small private income.

My friend, Jim, was one of those lovable, unassuming and caring people. In addition to being an amateur Egyptologist, musician and artist, he was an able philosopher, especially in the field of religion. As a student I had very little money to furnish the room he allowed me to use but his friendship at that time was of more value than riches for I was hurting inside.

It was not long before I had adopted my friend's Bohemian way of life. Quite often, assorted friends would gather there and we would talk, sometimes until three in the morning. We would cook breakfast, the friends would depart and we would make for our beds.

I entered into this new way of living with great zest, determined to blot out the recent hurts. This was the life in which I could forget the past and soak up my new freedom. How wrong I was. I was due for a rude awakening.

My discovery.

It was not long before I discovered that Jim was not only religious but rather overboard on Jesus Christ. I was a Christian but I liked all things in moderation. But the more I listened to him discourse on his faith and enjoy every moment of it at the same time, the more I desired what he had, and it grew as the days passed by. I was determined to be like Jim and set my sails accordingly.

Now prayer and Bible study were burdensome exercises that brought no real joy, but I thought to myself, if I am to succeed I must put every ounce of effort into trying. I would attack this problem in an all-out assault, and come what may, I would achieve my goal. I would be an equal alongside my friend. How I envied his knowledge of the Scriptures, and I assumed that he had broken all the prayer barriers. Yes, Jim radiated a real freedom – and I wanted it too!

My futile efforts.

So I created for myself a rigid schedule of prayer, Bible study and service. It was dreadful! Each night (or sometimes morning), I embarked on a two hour holy marathon. I filled the prayer time with confessing the sins I had committed that day, and to add a little padding, some of the sins for which I had already received forgiveness but still felt sorry for. If I didn't feel sorry, then I mentally agitated myself until I did. Then I would turn to my numerous prayer lists and drag my way through them, glancing at my watch at intervals wishing the stint away. Bible study was just as bad. I read my Bible for set periods of time, understanding very little of it but vainly hoping that some of it would stick. It was so tiring, but I was determined to keep at it. I had to become a really free Christian like Jim.

Serving was no better. I interpreted serving by doing good works and telling those around me how great God was and how bad they were. In the back of my mind I believed that the more I did, the more would God approve, and the greater would be my reward. I noticed that many of my friends seemed to steer away from me through that period, and it was much later that I came to hear of what a bore I had been. Poor souls!

Forced rhubarb.

It couldn't last, of course, and it didn't. It came to an end when some very patient soul suggested that I was rather like a rhubarb plant which had received a goodly portion of manure, then it had been covered over with an old bucket to help force it to grow. I felt humiliated after all the hard work I had put into becoming a real Christian . . . but he was right – absolutely right!

Jim's secret was not in the unorthodox life style he had adopted, but in the life he was freely receiving from God, and freely imparting to those around him. I had mistaken unconventionality for lack of concern, freedom for indifference. Jim was growing as his new nature intended him to grow – no manure and no covering bucket!

But what about us? What steps can we take to enjoy this new way?

God's way to grow – Five principles.

It will be helpful now if we consider five important principles. They are drawn from a simple allegory.

There was a gardener who planted an apple tree,

and he planted it where it would prosper best. The rain came, the sun shone, and the seasons passed; and the roots of the tree reached down into the good soil while its branches were lifted up to the sun and the sky. At the right season it blossomed, and the blossoms turned to fruit, and the fruit was good and sweet to the taste. The gardener was well satisfied.

If it will help you, think of the apple tree as the vine in John 15, but the principles of either allegory are the same. The five principles or lessons we draw from the allegory to help us grow into the likeness of Christ are these.

1. Let our roots reach down into the soil of his love.
2. Learn to be natural.
3. Become what you were intended to become.
4. Receive all that you are given.
5. As you receive freely, so give freely.

Shall we consider them in this order?

1. Let our roots reach down into the soil of His love.
Think of the tree being made up of two parts: the lower part, the roots, reaching down into the soil, and the upper part, the branches, leaves, flowers and fruit, stretching upwards and outwards towards the sky. Neither part can exist alone; each depends on the other. Nevertheless, it is the roots which do the searching; seeking out the water and nutrients to provide the vital sap for the upper part, which in turn, produces fruit as it benefits from the sun, rain and fresh air. Yes, the fruit is the evidence that the roots are functioning well.

Can we say with all honesty that we are bearing the fruit of the Holy Spirit which is love, joy, peace, patience, kindness, goodness, faithfulness, gentleness and self-control (Gal.5:22–23)? Most of us are aware of this deficiency, so we need to ask what we mean by searching, and just what are we searching for?

My personal interpretation of the allegory is something like this. The sap is the life and work of the Holy Spirit for He is the 'agent' of the Godhead who makes Jesus real to us. The soil is the means God makes available to us, such as the study of the Bible, prayer and meditation, and through them we receive His life. But the practice of these spiritual exercises is not so simple as we should like them to be, is it? So, may I suggest three simple guidelines that have helped me in my private times of searching.

(i) *It is for God we are searching.* King David once cried out, 'My heart says to thee, "Thy face, Lord, do I seek." ' (Psalm 27:8b) We commence our search with a cry from the heart; this is our prayer, and we do not move until it rises from within us. If we wait quietly on him, the blessed Holy Spirit will initiate this cry, for he helps us in our weaknesses, and he will intercede for us with sighs too deep for words (Rom.8:26). It is always a cause for joy to know that we are communing with the Lord, who is the giver of life.

(ii) *When we search, we expect to find.* This, our Christ promises us, for He has said, 'Ask, and it will be given you; seek, and you will find . . . for everyone who asks receives, and he who seeks finds' (Luke 11:9–10). Nothing could be clearer. However, if our motive is to accumulate knowledge or to become scholarly, then we may end up knowing a great deal about God without really knowing Him. We must take this truth to heart. God desires to meet with us more than we desire to meet with him. This should be of great encouragement to us.

(iii) *Giving ourselves to searching is an act of will.* Find a place where you will not be disturbed. If this is difficult, wait until you are lying in bed and the house is quiet. Think or quietly say to yourself something like this. 'This is my trysting place with my beloved Lord. Here He has promised to meet with me. I will turn away from the noise and bustle of this day, from my cares and duties, and I will turn my face to Him. I will drink of His life as I meditate on His greatness and majesty, and of His infinite compassion and understanding.' James 4:8 tells us that as we draw near to Him so He draws near to us. Hoping that something will happen is not enough; we must want it to happen. Take your time; make a practice of it. Do not give up if nothing seems to happen. You may be quite sure that He has drawn near to you – He always keeps His word. What you are learning is how to distinguish His presence and this is usually a gradual development. More often than not, you will recognise his presence in the deep stillness, and so, be still and know that He is God.

(iv) *Let us delight in what we find.* As we search for a richer and deeper appreciation of God, so will His Spirit lead us to discover many different and exciting finds. Each one will be a special treasure showing us who He is or what He has done. Don't rush; take each as it comes and delight in it so that it may stimulate a greater love and devotion.

2. *Learn to be natural.*

Some years ago, I read a statement made by a Christian leader in the U.S.A. which went something like this. 'God is who He says He is, and He can do whatever He says He can do. I am who God says I am, and I can do whatever God says I can do.' In other words, He is saying, 'Be natural!'

Unfortunately, this world confronts us daily with the teaching, 'You get nothing unless you pay for it.' If we are not careful it will be a simple matter to introduce this same teaching or philosophy into our faith. The truth is that there is nothing that we can do to merit more of God's love. He loves us – full stop! Of course we feel unworthy; of course there are times when we feel complete failures – but God continues to love us. We still remain his children. Healthy, natural growth commences with the acceptance of this truth. As we freely and joyfully search for Him in prayer and study, so He freely and joyfully imparts to us His life and forgiveness. It's as natural as breathing.

And so, let's be natural!

3. Become what you were intended to become.

Have you ever prayed a prayer like this? 'Lord, make me a fulltime worker for you, then I'll be so happy!' The truth is that you would not; not unless the Lord ordained it so – and you know it! I believe that you achieve true happiness when you are able to do absolutely nothing, and that with all quietness of soul, simply because it is what God wants.

Discovering what God wants us to become is more often a matter of loving patience and faithfulness on our part. God is not a dreamer but a realist, and it is in learning how to do well the ordinary daily chores in an attitude of caring that our spiritual exercises bring into clearer focus the will of God. If you were an apple tree in God's garden, then be well assured that at the appointed time you would bear apples. Stop trying to work out what you are to become, and simply enjoy being what you are now, but if He shows to you a particular direction, then walk that way with complete confidence.

4. Receive all you are given.

This is another of those statements we agree with in principle, but in practice, it's another matter.

John says to Bill, 'Look Bill, I've plenty of money and you're in need. I have here a hundred pounds in five pound notes. Now take them because I know that this is the amount you need.' Now, how does Bill reply? Usually, something like this. 'John, you really are generous . . . but no, I really couldn't . . . yes, I know you mean it . . . well, if you insist . . . but look, just a few pounds. I simply couldn't take more . . . you're too generous for words. Thank you . . . and I mean it!'

And so Bill leaves generous John with a fraction of what he could have had. Isn't it true to say that we are inclined to accept God's offers in a similar way? Should we not believe that He will offer us nothing at all unless He wants us to receive it? Not only this, however much He does offer us, that is the amount He wants us to take – because He knows that we need it. If a father knows how to give good gifts to his children, then God, our heavenly Father, knows how to give unstintingly to us (Matt.7:11).

5. *As you receive freely, so give freely*.

A healthy apple tree will produce good apples, but those apples are not for the tree, but for the gardener. In the right season it must shed its fruit to prepare itself for the following year. This is how things should be.

Now, if we receive freely of God's good strength, grace and abundance, we are certain to be good producers of holy fruit – love, joy, peace – and so on. But we must learn how to give this away to others freely, not counting the cost (Matt. 10:8b). If we keep it for ourselves it will go sour on us and become useless.

Giving is an essential part of living and growing. I've heard it said, and I believe it is true, that we cannot afford not to give. Even now I can see with great clarity Sir Tom Lees of the Post Green Community, standing on the platform at one of the Post Green Camps in Dorset, interpreting 2 Corinthians 9:7b as, 'God loves a hilarious giver!' – and He does!

The end result is worth it.

No doubt, there will be some who will say that all this sounds a little too easy to be true, and in one sense they will be right; we don't happen to be trees but people. Nevertheless, let us be fair, we do create many of our own problems or we create them for others. But as I have already said, God is not a dreamer; He is a realist; He knows our weaknesses, our frustrations and our inner longings, and always He gently woos us ever forward for there is a great and blessed future ahead of us. Do take time to consider what I am saying now. He has destined from the foundation of the earth, that we should grow up in every way into the likeness of Christ, his beloved Son (Eph. 4:15), and that on the day when He comes again we shall be like Him (1 John 3:2). Surely, that is worth contemplating. We shall look back on all our trials and tribulations and count them as nothing compared with what we have become and with what we have been given.

For the present, we may be assured that through every passing moment of the day God is at work in us by the agency of the Holy Spirit changing us into His likeness. If, during the process, we grow weary or afraid, or find ourselves for the umpteenth time flat on our faces, let us pause a moment and listen. We will hear His voice so full of compassion whispering to us: Come away by yourselves to a lonely place and rest awhile (Mark 6:31); I will never leave you nor forsake you (Heb. 13:5); for they who wait for me shall renew their strength, they shall mount up with wings like eagles, they shall run and not be weary, they shall walk and not faint (Isa.40:31).

A prayer for those who want to grow.

At this stage you might care to use some of the principles we have been discussing, especially if you seem to have experienced more defeat than victory, more failure than success, a spiritual deadness rather than a joyful life. You may, if it is convenient, sit quite still right now and think. Jesus is alive within you; he is all around you, enfolding you in his loving arms. Now, with a sincere heart breathe this simple prayer. For many it will be a prayer of reconfirmation.

Beloved Saviour, I am waiting in the stillness of your presence, drinking in the peace of your life, and offering myself to you just as I am. You alone know the thoughts and longings of my heart, and you alone can satisfy this thirst I have to become like you. I do want to grow into your likeness.

Give to me searching roots; roots to discover the beauty of your face and the compassion of your heart. Help me to be truly natural so that I may enjoy being surrendered, and let me walk the pathway of your choice.

I receive with grateful thanks every gift, every task and every mission, whether it brings joy or pain, knowing full well that you give nothing except you desire me to receive it for my good and for the glory of your Name.

And Lord, let me be the bearer of much precious fruit; fruit that will show that you are living your life in me to the full. And when all is done, Lord, freely take what is your own; even now I surrender it to you with joy, for all that I have and am is yours. Lord, I want to withhold nothing from you.

Please cover me with the mantle of your righteousness, and keep my feet on the pathway of your holiness. I ask all these things through your blessed name, Lord Jesus. Amen.

5: Amazing Love!

'See what love the Father has given us, that we should be called children of God; and so we are' (1 John 3:1). It takes but a few moments to realise what an astonishing statement this is. God's children – you and me! – sons and daughters of the Most High God! Little wonder the apostle John desires to exclaim the extraordinary nature of this love, for it is like no other.

What I find exciting is that God wants to develop this love-relationship with us. He cannot love us any more than he does which means that our primary task now is to learn how to receive His love so that we may love Him in return.

The longing to be loved by God.

I often prayed something like this: 'Oh Lord, if only I could know this love of yours in such a way that my life might be really transformed.' Of course, I knew that He did love me – the Bible said so, and all nature declared this to be a fact. What I longed for was to experience it as if He had placed His arms around me and I could hear the beating of His heart. Was I asking for too much? My friends seemed to think so. Rather solemnly they advised me to keep my feet on the ground and not to become too heavenly minded. I had tried to keep my feet on the ground for years but my heart had remained as wistful as ever – until one day in June 1983, when my prayer was answered.

Saturated with love.

I had been invited to speak alongside Dr. Jim Bigelow at one of the Rev. Jean Darnall's conferences for clergy and leaders at the centuries-old Carmelite centre, called 'The Friars', near Aylesford in Kent. We agreed that it should be a relaxed time so that we would be free to share our problems, pray for one another, and enjoy some pleasant times of fellowship. Jean, in her inimitable way, shared freely from her experiences and soon encouraged us to be as open as she was about the numerous and difficult problems confronting those with pastoral responsibilities. We talked and prayed not caring too much about the schedule, for a number of these good people were painfully exposing the hurts and disappointments of many years. By Wednesday evening of that week we had come to realise that considerable healing was needed. Deep down inside of me I felt something of their turmoil and anguish, and I longed to get away to be before the Lord. I had no idea what I wanted to ask Him; I simply wanted to be alone with Him. How else could I be of use to these people?

When everybody had finally turned in for the night and the noise of the evening had faded, I quietly left the guest house to wander alone wherever my feet would take me. There was a calming stillness over the ancient monastery buildings and I was conscious of the thousands before me who had sought the face of God in these hallowed grounds. Sadly, I found the doors to the chapels closed, and so I walked down the beautiful path that followed the River Medway, which, by the light of the moon, I discovered to be called the Rosary Way.

I was quieter now. I gazed at the glorious canopy of stars above me, marvelling at their complex patterns and brilliance. 'God, beloved God,' I cried, 'how can we doubt you? You do not change. Surely these stars are a testimony to your constancy and goodness!' I moved on a few paces and looked upwards once more . . . and then it came to me, so swiftly and surely. I cried out aloud this time not caring who heard me. 'Great and glorious God, we need to be saturated with your divine love! Your love is life; it transforms, energises, clarifies, heals! We come to you pleading to be loved, unaware that you desire to love us much, much more than we desire to receive your love.' Never before was I so determined to place myself at the disposal of the Lord to receive whatever He chose to give me.

Growing anticipation.

The guest house at 'The Friars' is built around a quadrangle with the lecture rooms, restaurant, and repository on the ground floor, and the bedrooms on the first floor. Fortunately, I had been allocated a corner room with two empty bedrooms on either side. It meant that I could pray aloud without disturbing a soul. I decided to be free of every kind of distraction, so I sat well back and relaxed in an old armchair with my feet resting on a smaller chair. Beside me I placed my Bible, notebook and pen should I need them. I heard the clock chiming in the distance and my watch confirmed that it was two in the morning; all was very normal.

I closed my eyes mulling over the conversation I had had with God, and as I did so, I knew without a shadow of doubt that His presence was all about me. I felt warm and happy, and just a little nervous. I opened my eyes and allowed myself to survey the room as it was. Nothing had changed; there was the wash basin, the crucifix on the wall, the green curtains at the windows and the rickety cupboard. I was wide awake yet wonderfully relaxed, but it seemed as if my body was lying on a cloud.

You know, in life there are moments when it is so difficult to believe God for anything, and there are the fewer times when you cannot fail to believe. There is no rational explanation but it is a valid and exciting experience when believing is as natural as breathing in the air around you. It was like that then.

The ecstasy of being loved.

From the depths of my being a cry arose, silent but purposeful. 'Dear Lord,' I cried, 'now . . . please love me! . . . I'm ready! . . . but, please Lord, only for a few moments!' I knew with such certainty that my body would be able to take only little of this kind of loving. How can I adequately describe what followed? It was as if the sluice gates to the vast reservoir of God's love were opened and I was engulfed by its waters that bore me upwards, ever upwards, into His arms of mercy and compassion. I shouted, rather bellowed, words I cannot remember, not aware or caring if I was disturbing the other guests. I rejoiced as His love penetrated, cleansed and freed my soul, my spirit, my mind; and for the first time in my whole life, I knew, as I could never know any other way, that I was really wanted, really accepted in the beloved, and would never be cast away. He wanted and loved me, not for what I did, but simply because I was the person I was. I knew all this with my whole being. It could not have lasted for more than ten to fifteen seconds. It was enough; I could have borne no more.

That night I slept in my Father's arms.

The love that will not let us go.

I learned so much as a result of that blessed experience, and some of the lessons I would like to share with you for your encouragement, and spiritual and mental enrichment. You do not have to have any great revelations or spiritual experiences to learn these lessons; only an earnest desire.

Years ago, I occasionally heard proclaimed with much fervour from the more evangelical pulpit a kind of warcry, 'You are saved to serve!' It was intended that Christians show their love for God through their service. This is only partly true. I think that God's call to all His children is, 'You are saved to be loved!'

If God so loves us as the Scriptures declare, then surely, the greatest pleasure we can give Him is the opportunity to love us. That seems reasonable, doesn't it? Have you ever considered how much the Lord, who loves us so deeply, longs for our time and attention in order to love us? Unfortunately, too often, we are too busy serving Him; we have to make sure that every moment of the day is filled with some activity or other. Even Bible study and prayer may become the means to escape being loved, and the yearning of God's heart remains unsatisfied.

God loves us that we might love him.

Our love for God will never grow and mature until we learn to be loved by Him. Yes, it does take time, and it is a very gentle process but so worthwhile. 1 John 4:10 says, 'In this is love, not that we loved God but that He loved us.' This is an important truth to grasp if we are to enter into the full freedom of Christian living. We cannot hope to love our brother, let alone the world, until we know how to consistently receive God's love. I sometimes advise people who long for this greater experience to give up formal praying for a while and give themselves wholeheartedly to being loved by the God of love. Some have said that this is wasting time, but I firmly believe that it is a good thing to 'waste' time on God.

Creative love.

There are some people who consider love in terms of the emotions being stirred. Now, while it is not a bad thing to have one's emotions stirred, it is much, much more than that. Love is a positive, creative and constructive force, whether it is God's love for man, or God's love in and through man. There is no real difference. God is the creator of all things, and God is love (Gen.1:1, 1 John 4:8), therefore, isn't it reasonable to assume that love is creative?

The creative and healing power of love.

Throughout the many years that I have been ministering to churches, communities and conferences, in this country and overseas, I have observed that whenever people choose to create and live in an environment of genuine love, that environment is conducive to healing. In its simplest form, the giving and receiving of love reduces tensions and stresses, encourages self-acceptance, which in turn releases people to the more natural processes of healing. But there are the occasions when the love of God is almost like an intelligent life-force. I suggest it is when we consciously identify with the will of God. Then, the environment of love is the place where God is able to minister the blessings of the Cross most effectively to those who are gathered in His Name (Matt. 18:20). Numbers do not matter; it could be just two people as in the case of David, the missionary and Peter, a young African lad.

A miracle of love.

Some years ago, on a small mission station in Central Africa, there lived and worked a small band of missionaries who knew the meaning of God's love. David and his wife, Jill, two of the missionaries, had taken into their care a young African boy whom they had named Peter. He was a sad casualty of a tribal raid. David and Peter became close friends and were often seen walking together with Peter wearing David's large wide-brimmed hat.

One day, it was diagnosed that Peter had contracted leprosy, and it was plain to all that the treatment he would need could be supplied only at the leprosarium some fifty miles away. David undertook the responsibility of breaking the news to him. It was with a very heavy heart that David took Peter aside to a place just outside the village where they had spent many happy times together. There they sat down and David prepared himself to break the awful news to Peter. There was a long silence which Peter could not understand. Then David spoke. 'Peter, I have to tell you something . . . you see . . . you have leprosy.'

David had no idea what the child's reaction would be. He sensed his confusion and dread, for everyone knew that lepers went to the leprosarium . . . and that was worlds away. He looked into the boy's face promising him faithfully that he would visit him often. A long, long silence followed. No words could express what they were feeling at that moment. And then, to the amazement of David, Peter looked straight into his face and said, 'Please, can I take your hat with me?'

In that moment it seemed that all the love in David welled up like a fountain. He picked up the boy and hugged him, and as he hugged him tears ran unashamedly down his face. Minutes later he put him down and, hand in hand, they returned to the village.

That night, Jill went to put Peter to bed. As she removed his clothes, she stopped, and stood there speechless. Every trace of leprosy had gone. Without a doubt it was the profound love that David had for Peter that brought about his healing. I know of similar instances where this has happened. Perhaps the love we have for others is having far more influence on them than we can imagine.

Consistent love.

That God loves us consistently is another delightful truth to keep in mind. Whether I am good or bad . . . He will go on loving me. Is that difficult to believe? Well, it's true! God cannot stop loving me because He is love; he cannot love me more or less – he can only love – perfectly! 'God so loved the world' (John 3:16) . . . and to this day, He has never stopped loving it. Does that mean that we can sin and get away with it? Of course not! What happens when we sin is not that God stops loving us, nor does He reduce His love in any way, but we harm ourselves by denying the benefits of His love until we seek His forgiveness.

Boundless love.

God's love is affected neither by time nor space; it is boundless. No matter to what depths of sin a person has fallen, no matter what his incapacity for helping himself, no matter in what state of despair he may find himself, no matter how broken or crushed, or rejected he may be, this pure, transforming love of God is able to reach him and raise him to unexpected heights.

How do we receive God's love?

It is one thing to know about God's love and that He desires us to receive it freely, but how is it done; what is the secret, if there is one? Frankly, I don't think there is anything secret about developing a love relationship. The ingredients are basically the same as when we develop human love relationships, namely, openness of heart, caring enough, and paying attention to those things that make the other person happy. Naturally, we think that it will be much more difficult to develop this relationship with God because we can see and talk to human beings face to face, but with God, we cannot –

He's invisible. But the possibility is always there if we keep in mind that God is real, not some vapour or mysterious energy.

The word 'spirit' often conjures up in the mind the sense of impermanence or indefinability, but this is far from the truth. This temporal world, and all pertaining to it, is ever passing away; it is transitory; but spiritual things, eternal things, comprise the true reality. We need to dwell on this fact before we begin. God is real. He is not a man, but yes, He is very real, loves His creation and desires to make Himself known to it. I find this encouraging.

Perhaps at this stage it would be helpful to consider the practice of making ourselves available to being loved by God. I will be drawing from my own personal experiences which I hope will be of help to you, but as you proceed, you will, no doubt, discover many more delightful truths and helpful ways. Do make a note of them afterwards.

1. We are meeting with the Most High God.
Don't allow this to frighten you, but do keep it before you. We are not meeting a casual friend or a neighbour, but the Lord of all creation – the Holy One. He wants us to meet with Him with pure hearts, free from sin; so let us spend some time examining ourselves, confessing our sins and receiving His forgiveness through Jesus Christ (1 John 1:9). It's a wonderful feeling to know that His holiness will not condemn us.

Meeting with a holy God doesn't mean that we have to be starchy and formal, but it does mean that we have to be reverent. A reverent Christian is a natural Christian; in other words, when we speak to Him we must be truly ourselves, fully aware that He knows every thought and every intention of the heart. False humility and flattery will avail us nothing, so let us keep things simple and truthful. Perhaps I should mention that much of the time will be spent in listening and receiving, so do not worry too much about what to say.

2. Place and time.
When we are to meet a special friend it's amazing how we always manage to make time for the occasion. Unfortunately, God, too often, gets the dregs of our time, and this may be because we have lost the sense of occasion and the nature of His being. So, it is helpful to arrange a time of mental preparation at some time prior to the meeting on these lines. This is not so much a prayer as a statement to yourself. 'Tonight, I'm going to meet with the Lord I love; the Lord who loves me more than I can ever appreciate. It will be a wonderful time together, and my heart is happy with anticipation for the moment when He covers me with His love. I will drink of the water of His divine life, and He will satisfy my soul's desire. Oh blessed Lord, I wait with eager longing to hear your voice. Thank you for inviting me.'

Not only fix the time (if you can), but also the place; your bedroom, the spare room, the attic, or even the shed in the garden. You will come then with greater expectation and you will not be disappointed.

3. Waiting with expectation.
Whatever place you select for your meeting, make sure you will be comfortable; this is vital. Choose a good armchair or spread some cushions on the floor so that you may lie, sit or kneel without any distraction or discomfort. And make sure, if possible, that you are not disturbed.

Once you are settled bodily, then settle your mind as well, putting away, by an act of will, all the distractions and problems of the day. Slowly and carefully read a favourite passage of Scripture that emphasises the goodness and love of God. Quietly consider its meaning in the light of your meeting with Him which is beginning to take place. Place your Bible to one side and rest.

Drink in the stillness and allow your heart, mind and soul to reflect on the wonder of this remarkable moment. I sometimes say, 'Here I am, in the presence of my Lord of love. He who made the heavens and the earth; He who is all beauty, all that is good and wonderful; He who has given His life for me, who loves me with an everlasting love, is now filling this room with His presence. He has kept His promise to come to me if I will come to him (James 4:8). I willingly and gladly open myself now, this moment, to receive Him.'

There are no words to describe the exquisite nature of this expectation that may fill the whole being. It is an expectation which may begin to grow the moment you fix the time and place, but it is heightened if you dwell on it through the day as would a person who is in love.

4. Bathing in his love.

It is a truly remarkable love that the Lord has for us; it is pure, holy and truthful. It should be the most natural thing in the world for a Christian to receive it; as natural as breathing in good fresh air. I find it helpful to use my natural senses to stimulate my supernatural senses; my mind to stimulate my spiritual awareness. I raise my arms to Him and whisper the holy Name of Jesus. I bid Him welcome, and like the two disciples on the road to Emmaus, invite Him to stay with me. I can only say that as I imagine the presence of Jesus gathering me into Himself, my spirit is made acutely aware of an indescribable warmth, a profound sense of being wanted for myself, a peace, that is almost tangible. I have come home, but I am still on earth. The desire to pray has gone; there is no longer any need. I can come no closer to Him for He has drawn me as near to Himself as it is possible while I still inhabit this body. All I can do is marvel that He should love me so.

A word of guidance and encouragement.

What I have described is what can happen but certainly not every occasion is so remarkable. Our problem is adjusting our minds and thinking to what God says. Sometimes, I have to speak aloud to myself (I find it helpful). I say, 'Denis, you're having a problem with believing. Now, who are you going to believe, God or your feelings? Has he stopped loving you because you don't feel loved?' Of course, I have to affirm God's love for me in spite of my negative feelings – how can I deny Him? It helps me to look upwards once again. This is not a case of mind over matter but simply stating what is, and in so doing, we encourage our minds to agree with God. Try it and see for yourself.

Other debilitating factors may be domestic pressures, poor health, business difficulties and the like. They certainly may affect our spiritual and mental vitality, and consequently, our response to God's loving advances. But, remember, He is gracious and understands us far more than we understand ourselves, so don't give up. Be a little more gentle with yourself. Learn how to surrender yourself to His cocooning love. Don't talk! Simply rest your whole being in His loving embrace – imagine it happening. Whatever He wants to happen to you will happen in His own good time; He is in no hurry. Allow the minutes to pass by, for what is time when we are dwelling where it meets with eternity.

Our love response.

If we could measure in terms of human wealth the value of our encounter with God, then such a treasure could never be realised. Only in eternity could this be known. You see, the Cross of Christ alone can express the magnitude of God's love for us, and I find that when I meditate on this awesome truth, that God loves me this much, I am lost for words; there is nothing I can do, only stand amazed. I am deeply sorry that I have caused Him so much suffering but it is a sorrow mixed with joy through the forgiveness I have received. All too soon the moment passes but His love can never pass away. We are now of this world and our love response to God, if it is to have any real meaning, must be a love response to those we rub shoulders with day by day.

Showing forth His love.

After all that I've said, please don't think that I mean that from now onwards there will be no more troubles, no more problems, no more inner struggles. They are part of life itself and we cannot, and must not avoid them. However, as we regularly take the time and trouble to make ourselves available to the loving ministrations of God, so our love for Him will grow, and so too will our love for our fellow men. Dutiful service will gradually become an act of worship, for through our neighbour, enemy as well as friend, we shall behold the face of God.

In the last chapter we considered the five principles of growing as Christians; in this, we have discovered growth's most vital ingredient – love. This is the evidence the world craves to experience, but it can only experience it through you and me. Every day is an opportunity to show clearly the glory and love of Christ, but we need to maintain and strengthen our lifeline and this is only possible as we regularly turn aside and come into the secret place of the Most High.

Perhaps you will find the following prayer helpful if you feel the need to strengthen your relationship with God, or even confirm your faith.

Holy Father, I have longed to love you so much more than I do. I have tried, but I seem to fail more than succeed. The paths of duty and service are often hard and thorny. The refreshment is there but I don't always find it, and so I turn to you, Father, for help and guidance.

I realise more than ever that I must set time aside in order to meet with you, and you with me, and this I will do with your help. Please give to me, with the help of your Holy Spirit, the courage and determination to allow nothing to deflect me from this pathway of discovery. Let every distraction and obstacle be subject to your control. And please, gracious Lord, stir up within me such a spirit of expectancy that it will not be satisfied until we meet and I rest in your arms of love. There, may I drink the fullness of your life; there, may my soul be consumed by your love.

Then, Father, when I hear the call, 'Whom shall I send?' I will gladly reply, 'Here am I! Send me.'

All these things I ask in the Name of your Son, Jesus Christ. Amen.

6: The Glory of God Within Us.

It will become apparent that growing into God's likeness and surrendering ourselves to His love will require application and patience on our part, but the time and effort spent will be worth it. It must have a profound effect on us. It certainly improves our attitudes, our hopes and aspirations, and our longing to be fully given to Him, To put it another way, we experience subtle changes for our minds are being renewed. To have a renewed mind doesn't mean that we simply think good and beautiful thoughts. What the Bible seems to imply is a thorough change of the mind so that we are enabled to think God-thoughts with a childlike simplicity (Rom. 12:2). In this book we shall be learning some of the ways to develop a God-awareness in our thinking, how to agree with His plan and purpose, and how to identify with His will. These disciplines are important for they shape and condition our appreciation and love for God to the extent that we are more able to become channels of His love to others.

What the Bible also explains is that this renewal of the mind produces in our spirits a 'transformation'. It was as I pondered this word which described the work of change in us a little more carefully, that I realised, really for the first time, what honoured people we are. One nineteenth-century commentator explained the transformation this way. 'The verb is the same as that used in the account of our Lord's Transfiguration, and it may be noted that it is used of the transformation of the Christian into the likeness of Christ. The process originates with the Lord and is a spiritual power and presence working upon our spirits.'

A remarkable statement, indeed! We are actually being transformed into the likeness of Christ. What does this mean to us, personally? What is it that is happening within us? I have been so encouraged seeking the answers that I want to share my observations and deductions with you.

The Cathedral incident.

My enquiry began when I read through some old papers relating to certain happenings in 1962 at the Prince Rupert Cathedral in Canada. They had been written by a Church Army sister who had visited the then Dean Pattison of the cathedral. I had the privilege of meeting the Dean for a very short while when he visited the U.K. During their conversation he spoke of the manner in which the Holy Spirit had moved on them, how he and his fellow priests had been wonderfully anointed and some had spoken in new languages.

What attracted my attention was the reference to the ministry directed to three young people – two women and a man. The Dean said that when he and his priests laid hands on them, on each occasion, they spoke with a new tongue and a circle of light appeared on their foreheads which seemed to glow from within – very clear at first and seen by all – gradually becoming diffused around them. All now are in God's service.

A symbol of holiness.

When I first read this account I remember experiencing certain doubts, but then, after reflecting on the integrity of the Dean and his fellow priests, I must admit that I became a little excited. I reminded myself of the centuries of classical paintings and the manner in which the artist had clearly depicted the holiness of a person by encircling his head with a halo. It could be a simple affair or a complex pattern, but it was intended to make the statement that from the inner part of that person God's glory shone, unseen to the ordinary eye.

Although the Church adopted the practice from the third and fourth centuries, the Hellenistic period, one cannot help wondering if such people, as the God-fearing Fra Angelico, were enlightened by God to witness this phenomenon on certain subjects they painted. Of course, these are only my reasonings, but they started me searching. If the young people at the Prince Rupert Cathedral actually exhibited the holy light of God shining from within them, then, what is God saying to us, and what do the Scriptures say?

God in us.

The Scriptures that challenged me afresh on that occasion were those I had considered in an academic way for college studies or for sermon preparation. Now I was more concerned about knowing what they really meant. I was anxious to receive all God could give me.

> If the Spirit of him who raised Jesus from the dead dwells in you . . . then he will give life to your mortal bodies, also through his Spirit which dwells in you.
>
> (Rom. 8:11)

Remarkable! God wants me to have the same life as Jesus. Not at some time in the future when I get to heaven, but now! Also, it resides in my mortal body.

> But he who is united with the Lord becomes one spirit with him.
>
> (1 Cor. 6:17)

Again, this is a statement which defies adequate explanation. The Spirit of the Almighty and Most Holy God unites His Spirit with mine! What incalculable effects must this have on me? Then, as if needing to emphasise the importance of this truth, he adds a note of grave warning:

> Do you not know that your body is a temple of the Holy Spirit within you, which you have from God? You are not your own; you were bought with a price. So glorify God in your body.
>
> (1 Cor. 6:19–20)

There are other Scriptures I could quote, and all of them seem to be saying, 'God is at work in you, both day and night, transforming you into the likeness of Jesus.' Maybe we can accept this as fact, but what does it mean He is really doing? What sort of change is taking place? Would it be wiser to shelve the whole business in case we lean towards a too literal interpretation? In all honesty, I don't think we can. If God takes pains to show us His truth, whatever it is, we must at least try to understand what He is saying, otherwise, we may miss out to our detriment. If our search is one of truth and not from mere curiosity, then His Spirit has promised to be our guide and teacher (John 16:13–14).

Shekinah glory.

The Church borrowed the word Shekinah from the Jews to express the visible majesty of the Divine Presence. It is not found in the Bible and it means 'to rest', 'to dwell' or 'to settle'. In the Old Testament the Divine Presence was seen to rest or dwell on the mercy-seat which was situated between the cherubim in the Tabernacle, and later, in the Temple. It must have been a glorious sight. The Jews use the word, especially in their sacred Targums, as an alternative for the name of God which they hold with such high regard and reverence. The

Shekinah was present whenever God was said to be dwelling with His people, Israel, and it is from this aspect, of dwelling with His people, that we are going to consider the most important of the Scriptures relating to His glory. Our conclusions will be illuminating.

The pillar of cloud and of fire.

Now the Lord made His glory first appear when Israel left Egypt by way of the Red Sea.

> And the Lord went before them by day in a pillar of cloud to lead them along the way, and by night in a pillar of fire to give them light that they might travel by day and by night; . . . they did not depart from before the people.
>
> (Exodus 13:21–22)

The strange thing about this phenomenon was that it gave light to the Israelites but it was a 'cloud of darkness' to the Egyptian hosts (Exodus 14:24). Or it might be expressed this way. The fiery appearance of the Deity shone forth from the cloud and by its amazing brightness confounded them.

The glory at Sinai.

When the Israelites arrived at Sinai the glory was removed for a while for God was to speak to Moses on the mountain top. After they had thoroughly cleansed themselves, for the mountain was holy beyond all imagination, God came in terrible might and power. A thick impenetrable cloud appeared over the mountain and the assembled people trembled with fear as the awe-inspiring trumpet of God broke the silence, growing ever louder, and peals of thunder shook the place where they stood, and from the thick cloud shafts of dazzling light issued forth eclipsing the light of day (Exodus 19:7–25).

The Lord was visiting his people Israel in Shekinah glory.

Two other observations we make concerning this glory on Sinai. The first is when Moses and his fellow elders ascend the mountain and God reveals Himself to them.

> And they saw the God of Israel; and there was under his feet, as it were, a pavement of sapphire stone, like the very heaven for clearness.
>
> (Exodus 24:10)

The second is when Moses leaves them to ascend further up the mountain to receive the tablets of stone on which are written the law and the commandments.

> Now the appearance of the Lord was like a devouring fire on the top of the mountain in the sight of the people of Israel.
>
> (Exodus 24:17)

There, in the presence of the Lord, Moses stayed forty days and returned having undergone an astonishing change. The glory had been so intense that he had received it into his bodily self.

> Moses did not know that the skin of his face shone because he had been talking with God. And when Aaron and all the other people of Israel saw Moses, behold, the skin of his face shone, and they were afraid to come near him . . . (so) he put a veil on his face.
>
> (Exodus 34:30–33)

I can see no reason to doubt this actually happened, and if it did, how must the light of Christ, who has made His dwelling place in us by faith, be affecting and changing us. I am reminded of a moving story from Arthur Blessitt's book, *Turned on to Jesus*, when he was invited to preach at the First Bijou Church in Lake Tahoe on the Nevada-California state line.

Christ by the lake side.

One evening, Arthur Blessitt and his friend, Ron Willis, agreed to wander by the lake side for a time of prayer and sharing. It was bitterly cold and giant snowdrifts made their progress difficult. As they walked, their conversation turned to Peter, of his great faith when his Lord called him to walk on the water and of the moment when he doubted. Arthur criticised him for doubting but admired his courage, perhaps wondering what he would have done under the circumstances. Soon, they could go no further, their path impeded by a snowbank, and the mist was beginning to drift in from the lake. Frozen and with teeth chattering they headed back the way they had come. It was then that they saw Jesus.
Arthur Blessitt tells the story.

'He was there!
Christ!
Standing on the water!
I shook my head in disbelief and turned away. Ron had his back to the lake. I didn't say a word to him. When he turned toward the water, he said,
"Arthur, have you looked out over the lake?"
"Yes, I saw Him too, Ron, what's happening?"
I looked again.
Him!
There still
Unmistakably there.
And now He came walking toward us.
His garment was white as a flourescent lamp, glistening, shining and sparkling, so immaculate and pure that it looked more silver than white.'

So unworthy!

Arthur tells how he and Ron fell to their knees overwhelmed by their unworthiness and lack of purity. He continues:

> 'Then all of a sudden, I was suffused with peace, as if he were saying everything is all right.
> He was coming closer, walking slowly toward us.
> Closer and closer.
> The nearer He came, the greater the joy and peace I felt welling inside me.
> It seemed as if I were beginning to float out to Him, as Peter had.
> Then He stopped.
> He stood and looked at us.
> If he had taken another step I think two bodies would have been found on the shore the next morning. Ron and I would have gone to be with Him.'

He further relates how he felt waves of power engulfing him together with a remarkable increase of faith and love. Nothing could describe the precious moments of union with the Lord.

'You've been with Jesus!'

Later, they discussed how they would break the news to their wives whom they were soon to meet. They went first to the motel where Arthur and his wife, Sherry, were staying. Arthur takes up the story.

> 'I had forgotten the key to our motel room. When I knocked, Sherry opened the door, took one look at me . . . and screamed! Then she backed away, her hands shielding her face. Sherry said,
> "You've been with Jesus!"
> "But . . . but . . . how could you know?"

"Your face, Arthur, it's glowing! It's radiant!"
On the ride to Ron's house, Sherry wouldn't sit next to me. She stayed in the back seat. I was incapable of comforting her while she sobbed.'

The same reaction had come from Ron's wife, Barbara. Ron found her in their bedroom when he got home, and Barbara wouldn't touch or go near him.

' "There's a glowing light around your face," Barbara had said. Ron and I looked at each other. I noticed nothing different about him, nor he about me.'

Arthur Blessitt comments that he did not expect anyone to believe his story because it goes beyond logic and rational explanation. I suggest that Moses' encounter with God on Sinai creates a valid precedent for accepting Arthur Blessitt's story, and as we shall see, there are some important supporting Scriptures in the New Testament.

The glory of the Tabernacle.

When Moses finally returned from his meeting with God on Sinai, he brought with him explicit and detailed instructions concerning the preparation and erection of the Tabernacle. With the giving of the Law and the commandments a new way of life was to begin, and the Tabernacle was to become the focal place where God would meet with His people. When Moses finished the work, the book of Exodus tells us, 'Then the cloud covered the tent of the meeting, and the glory of the Lord filled the Tabernacle. And Moses was not able to enter the tent of meeting, because the cloud abode above it, and the glory of the Lord filled the Tabernacle' (Exodus 40:34–35).

The glory of the Temple.

The Tabernacle was to be only a temporary dwelling place until the great Temple had been erected in King Solomon's time. By all accounts it must have been astonishingly beautiful.

In 2 Chronicles 5 we read how Solomon assembled all the people for the grand dedication day. The ark was brought up from the city of David to find its permanent lodging place under the covering of the cherubim in the Holy of Holies. When all was ready, each person at his appointed place and the fever of preparation over, the signal was given. To the swelling clarion notes of the six score of silver trumpets, the finely trained voices of the Levitical singers were raised. And when these, with all the instrumentalists, poured forth their praise and thanksgiving with one heart and mind . . . ' "for He is good, for His steadfast love endures forever", the house, the house of the Lord, was filled with a cloud, so that the priests could not stand to minister because of the cloud; for the glory of the Lord filled the house of God' (2 Chron. 5:13–14).

How can any person find suitable words to describe such an occasion! But memories are short, for as generations passed, the extraordinary deteriorated to become mundane and familiar. The glory of the Lord departed. The long wait had begun.

Glory means presence and holiness.

If we made an extensive study of the Old Testament and considered every other passage where God's glory appeared, it would not be too difficult to make these observations.

1. Wherever the glory is, there too must be God's presence.

2. Such glory is visible evidence that God dwells within it, for it proceeds from Him.

3. From the Old Testament Scriptures we have considered, it is a sign that He is dwelling in the midst of His people.

4. No one may come near without the qualification of holiness – for God is holy.

The glory of Christ.

When God visited His people, Israel, once more, it was through His Son Jesus Christ. He made this truth clear when on the banks of the Jordan, after Jesus had risen from His baptism, He declared, 'This is my beloved Son in whom I am well pleased' (Matt. 3:17).

The fact that God was abiding in Christ was demonstrated to Peter, James and John when, before their eyes, He was transfigured so that, 'his face shone like the sun, and his garments became white as light' (Matt. 17:2).

God, the Father, in Jesus, had come to dwell in His people, but sadly we read that they would not receive Him (John 1:11), and so, He gathered to Himself the few who would, gave to them His life, and called them God's sons (John 1:12). Later, at the Last Supper, He told them, 'If a man loves me, he will keep my word, and my Father will love him, and we will come to him and make our home with him' (John 14:23).

What could be clearer? God dwells in those who love Him. He makes them a holy people. God's splendid glory must be in us. We are His dwelling place, His temple. Unseen to mortal eyes, there is a glory which shines out from the indwelling Christ in us to the world at large. Unlike the people in the Old Testament days, who stood well away from God's presence because of His holiness, we are invited to become His dwelling place through the mediation of Christ our Saviour.

We are being metamorphosed.

There is a word that occurs only four times in the New Testament. It is the Greek word which when used in the

English form translates as 'metamorphosis'. It is made up of two parts, 'meta' – to change, and 'morph' – form, or in other words, 'to change the form'.

Biologists tell us that in the higher insect orders, such as butterflies and moths, the larvae undergo a process of metamorphosis where much of the body is disorganised and then reorganised. To protect the creature it is encased in a cocoon or chitinous chrysalis. It is a remarkable phenomenon.

Now the Bible tells us that we are being metamorphosed into the likeness of Jesus. That is the Greek word used. Does it mean just a change of moral character for the better as Romans 12:2 might imply, or is it a process which defies any rational explanation? The three words used to translate the Greek for metamorphosis into English are, 'transfigure' (Matt. 17:2; Mark 9:2), 'transform' (Rom. 12:2), and 'change' (2 Cor. 3:18). Let us consider them in turn.

Transfigure.
Matthew 17:2 and Mark 9:2 relate the occasion when Jesus took Peter, James and John with Him to a mountain (perhaps Tabor or Hermon), and there before them He was transfigured; the divine glory flowed out into visible brightness. He remained quite human, but His face shone with all the brilliance of the sun. Notice too, His actual clothes became as white as light. His glory differed from that of Moses in that Moses' glory was received from God in whose presence he had stayed, but the glory of Jesus was His very own.

Transformed
Romans 12:2 is our next Scripture. It marks the difference between outward conformity and an inner change. St Paul is encouraging a continuing process of transformation so that the excellencies and perfection of Christ might be seen. This is achieved by an inner renewal

of the mind and by resistance to the influence which characterises this age.

'Transform' here may well be understood to mean 'the change of moral character for the better', but, in addition, the true renewal of the mind will produce an intrinsic change within us, thus promoting the metamorphosis we have been discussing.

Changed.

We now come to an extremely interesting use of the word – 'changed'.

> And we all [not some of us] with unveiled face, beholding the glory of the Lord, are being changed into His likeness from one degree of glory to another; for this comes from the Lord who is the Spirit
>
> (2 Cor. 3:18)

This verse must be considered in the context of the preceding passage from verse four of the chapter. The writer, with great care, lays the foundation for interpreting its meaning by telling us of the differing glories of the old and new covenants. The old covenant was born in glory when Moses, on Mount Sinai, received the written code in the presence of God. In the process he was changed so that his face shone with such splendour that it required him to cover it in the presence of the Israelite people. However, this glory was an absorbed glory and it began to fade, reflecting the nature of the covenant itself which could not give life, but rather, only condemn man to death when he sinned. But, thanks be to God, this was to last only until the perfect covenant had been ratified by Jesus Christ.

A surpassing glory.

This new covenant has a surpassing glory of such magnitude that when it is compared with the glory of the old covenant, it makes it appear to fade into insignificance – such is the contrast. The reason? Well, it is a covenant of forgiveness and life. This glory cannot fade because Jesus Christ comes to live and make His home in the believer's heart. It is an indwelt glory through the indwelling Christ. The whole body of Christian believers, outside of place and time, is a beautiful anti-type of the Tabernacle, and (in the more permanent sense) the Temple, in which the Shekinah glory of God rests or dwells.

In passing, may I express an opinion concerning the glory exhibited by Arthur Blessitt. I think it possible that this was a combination of absorbed glory shining out and an inner-activated glory by reason of the Spirit of Christ indwelling him.

God's glory in us.

What should all this mean to us – the Church in the twentieth century?

Returning once more to 2 Corinthians 3:18, we notice that St Paul is using the phrase 'are being changed'. This implies an ongoing, moment-by-moment process. Verse 18, then, is saying something like this. 'All of us, who have Christ within us, have no need to veil our faces. We are gazing on His glory as if reflected in a mirror, and this is, moment by moment, metamorphosing us in ever-increasing splendour into His very own image.'

I appreciate only too well that what we have been discussing may be difficult for some of us to believe, but how else can we rightly interpret the Scriptures we have considered? This is a message of encouragement and hope and I find it greatly uplifting. Such is the desire of God to draw us closer to Himself; such is His desire that we learn to wait on Him, to listen to the beat of His heart, to know His will and voice. He has come, Father, Son and Holy Spirit, to make His home in us, to enjoy our fellowship, to lavish on us the gifts that only He can give. Surely, apart from the Cross there can be no greater demonstration of His love for us. If we could but set aside our doubts and fears, and offer to Him our minds, our thoughts, our reasonings, to be so renewed, then we could, with childlike innocence, behold the transforming beauty of His face. This is what stimulates union with God. This is how we become lights to the world.

Only Peter, James and John beheld the visible glory of Jesus, and few may have seen this glory in the Church. But it is there. And what will the glory be when the Bridegroom comes for His Bride, no longer a tabernacle that moves through the wilderness of this life, but an eternal temple in the heavens above? Surely, we should be humbled by the thought of such grace being poured out on us.

> O come, let us worship and bow down, let us kneel
> before the Lord, our Maker, for he is our God.
> (Psalm 95:6–7b)

A prayer of acknowledgement and commitment.

Lord, Most High God; King, most glorious, how can I begin to thank you for the privilege of being your child. As I meditate on this divine transformation that is taking place within me, on the ever-increasing splendour which is the fruit of your Spirit's work, and on the promise that I am being changed into your likeness, my heart is filled with gratefulness and praise.

And this I pray, O Lord of Glory, that I may be so given to you, and my mind so renewed, that through my life and service, the world may see the beauty of your perfection, the light of your loveliness and grace, and the power of your resurrection life.

Therefore, Lord, show me how to walk closer with you; teach me how to wait on you, how to listen to that still, small voice. Anoint my spiritual eyes and ears so that I may better understand the things that really please you. I desire that closeness, that reverent intimacy, for deep within me, in spite of my many failings, there is a cry for union with you.

I thank you for your unfailing promises, the encouragement of your holy word, and your peace which passes all understanding. These prayers I humbly offer to you in the Name of Jesus Christ, my Saviour. Amen.

7: Our Unique Father.

It is not everyone who can appreciate the memories of a good and loving father. Some will tell you that all they can remember is ill-treatment, rejection, or just plain neglect. They were born into this world with a longing to be loved but have grown up embittered and disillusioned by the treatment they have received. Fortunately, there is the happier side with stories of faithfulness and caring, and even sacrifice when the need arose. But no matter how much a man may excel in exercising his role and duties as a father he can never attain to the excellence and uniqueness of the fatherhood of God.

Now this, at first, may appear to be rather intimidating, almost as if God is a sort of super-father who gazes down on us from His superior position in heaven above, and waits to judge and punish our every misdeed. This is far from the truth! What perfect fatherhood means is that there are no depths of sin, misery or despair that we may sink to but His heart is reaching down to those same depths with us, and that when we turn to Him in our distress, He joyfully receives us back into His arms of love, and then reinstates us as though we had never been away from Him. Now, that is perfect fatherhood. Can you think of any human father who would go to those lengths?

Here is an example reflecting this love at the more imperfect human level.

A Post Green Camp.

Lytchett Minster is a small village in the county of Dorset, not too far from the seaside town of Bournemouth. Half a mile to the north of the village is Post Green, the gracious home of Sir Thomas and Lady Lees. For many thousands of people, this name conjures up not only the idea of community life, but more especially, wonderful memories of camps and conferences. At the time of which I speak, my wife, Florence Mary and I were associated with the work there, and for us, the annual camps were one of the highlights of the year.

It was the last night of a Bank Holiday camp and the crowds had gathered in the marquee for a time of celebration and praise. After a time of singing and spontaneous worship, David Mills, one of the camp leaders, invited people to come forward to share their experiences of how they felt that God had spoken to them. They were not at all slow in making their way to the platform. Young and old, in their turn, shared their tales of newly-found love for God, of decisions they had made, and even how some families had been re-united. It was impossible not to be stirred.

The odd young man.

Then it was Alan's turn. He stood some moments in silence before the microphone. Desperately he was searching for the right words. Everybody was responding sympathetically to this odd young man with the strange haircut and peculiar assortment of clothes. Nervously, the words slipped from him.

'I didn't want to come to this camp. I didn't know what to expect . . . but my friends said they were going. Well, I had nothing better to do . . . so I came . . . with them, of course! Well, it was all religious, and at first I just wanted to get away . . . but I stayed.'

He gazed down at the crowd, pausing to consider what to say next.

'You see, my mum died some time ago, and my dad brought us up. He was so good but I gave him a hard time. We had lots of rows because I used to come in late at night. He didn't like the way I dressed and my language . . . but I didn't care! I wanted him off my back! Well, it went on for some while like this . . . then I decided to go – clear off . . . so I took to the road.'

Clearly Alan did not want to describe what followed, but he took courage, and raising his head he continued.

'The months that followed I'd rather not talk about, except that I fell lower and lower and got mixed up in every kind of rotten thing possible. I knew that I couldn't ever go back home again. Most of my friends had left me . . . I just wanted to die!' Then, a gentle smile illuminated his face and he looked down at some young fellows sitting in the front seats, and said, 'These guys brought me here . . . and do you know what? I've become a Christian!'

Suddenly, the crowded tent was filled with shouts of praise and the clapping of hands. The noise subsided but there could be heard in the far part of the marquee a cry to be followed with sobbing. Alan continued.

'I just wish I could have my life over again . . . but I don't think my dad would ever want to see me again.'

He's my son!

A shout was heard, indistinct. Again it was from the far part of the marquee. Alan stopped speaking. The crowd turned to identify the cause of the disturbance, but Alan's eyes, now wide with astonishment, were fastened on a middle-aged man who was racing to the platform. Tears were flowing freely down his cheeks, and as he came he shouted, 'I'm his father . . . and he's my son! Oh yes, I want him back again!'

There could not have been a dry eye anywhere as

those two estranged persons became father and son once more.

If this is for you a moving story of a human father's love for his son, how much greater is the perfect love of a perfect father, namely, our God, for His children. The discovering of the magnitude and nature of our heavenly Father's love for us is something to which we should give our attention.

The most beautiful relationship known to man.

Long before man inhabited this earth, a relationship existed that had no beginning. It was the divine Father-Son relationship. The fact that the Son of God was begotten of the Father implies that He pre-existed with the Father. Indeed, He was God (John 1:1).

In the plan and purposes of God, He ordained to employ this relationship to populate our earth in an orderly fashion. But what I find so meaningful is that it was not merely a means of procreation, but through the parental and filial love-ties of the human families born, we are more able to see and appreciate the nature and love of the God who made us. I must add here, that when I speak of the father-son relationship, I understand it in the wider sense of the father-mother-son-daughter relationship. Consider the mother and father who proudly hold their new child to themselves, and one catches a glimpse of our Father in heaven treasuring His only Son, Jesus – and us! No wonder it meant so much to Him when He released Him to become the Saviour of the world. What love He must have for us! What pain and suffering He had to bear! No, our God is never cold and calculating, waiting to make us suffer for every offence we commit, but He is slow to become angry and so quick to show His mercy. His greatest joy is to forgive the sinner and to encourage His children to greater love, for Himself, and for one another.

An intimate and growing relationship.

Imagine a father and a son who have great love and respect for one another. The father owns a large estate and has allocated the responsibility for part of it to the son. Every so often they gather together in the father's office to discuss the latest developments and proposals for the benefit of the estate. The father has had years of experience in estate management, while the son is always willing to learn more.

The father, aware of his son's limitations, accepts the overall responsibility, but at the same time, knowing that his son can only learn through experience, gives him the freedom to make his own decisions. However, being a caring father, he is always available for guidance and help, and on some occasions, he may even veto a decision. Naturally, the father is concerned for the prosperity of the farm, but he is even more concerned that his son becomes a man after his own heart. He wants him to grow in integrity, knowledge and skill; a man he can be proud of – because he loves and respects him.

The son, on the other hand, does not look on himself as a serf or a common servant, but as a responsible son. He enjoys his happy and relaxed relationship with his father, but he does not take advantage of this. He sets himself to learn how to do his job well, not merely for self-satisfaction, but because he is aware that it makes his father happy. His one desire is to grow into his father's likeness, and so, he freely shares with him his troubles, his successes, his ideas and hopes, trusting in the consistency of his father's love.

This is the kind of relationship that our Father wishes to enjoy with us.

A perfect relationship.

The love that our Father has for His Son, Jesus Christ, is the same love that He has for each one of us. It is a perfect relationship. You see, God is a God of absolutes. He is absolute righteousness, absolute holiness, absolute peace, absolute love; He cannot be more or less than what He is. This means that He cannot love us, his children, more than He does, nor less than He does. He doesn't say to the 'super-saints', 'You've really succeeded, not like those failures over there! So, you'll enter into into my grade "A" relationship.' No, every child of God has precisely the same opportunity of belonging to Him, and entering into the happy discovery of what it means to have such a treasure of a Father as God.

Now, let us interpret first the allegory from our Father's standpoint, and then from ours as His children. (Needless to say, by sons I mean sons-daughters.)

Our Father's great concern for us.

We have a gracious Father of whom we may say with King David, 'Thine, O Lord, is the greatness, and the power, and the glory, and the victory; for all that is in the heaven and in the earth is thine' (1 Chron. 29:11). His estate is boundless and eternal, and it is into His kingdom that we are born as sons (John 1:12–13). We may not be clever or very wise as far as this world is concerned, but He has made up for this by giving us His own wisdom, righteousness, sanctification and redemption (1 Cor. 1:26–30).

Now as sons we are expected to take our places in the activity of the kingdom. We are commissioned to tell others His good news, and to teach them what we ourselves have received (Matt. 28:19–20), endeavouring at all times to lead lives worthy of such a great calling (Eph. 4:1); for what we are actually doing is possessing, or inheriting the kingdom (1 Cor. 6:9, 2 Thess. 1:5). It is certainly a challenge to realise that God trusts us with His property, and even more so when we remember that

He is expecting a return on what is entrusted (Matt. 25:14–29).

However, of this we may be sure. He appreciates our weaknesses and anxieties, and says to us, 'Look, children, just get on with my work and I'll look after your needs, and all those things you cannot handle' (Matt. 6:25–34). 'Only give me the opportunity. That's a fair offer, isn't it?' In addition, His office is always open for consultation. It will become evident that He is never too busy to listen to the smallest problem so that we may go away comforted and strengthened.

A Father worth loving and serving.

Briefly, we have tried to view sonship from our Father's standpoint, and what He may expect of us. Now let us see how we may view the Father in terms of our response. In a nutshell we could say that He is a Father who deserves our undivided love, attention and commitment. Nothing is too good for Him; nothing is too great. His first-born Son, Jesus, has shown us the way so that we, with humble hearts, may joyfully follow in His footsteps.

In the Scriptures we are encouraged to exhort one another, to lift one another up especially when we are flagging. Here are three exhortations I wish to share with you for they contain the essence of active sonship.

1. Let us walk as God's sons.
2. Let us live in the spirit of sonship.
3. Let us delight in our fellowship with God.

1. Let us walk as God's sons.
We are not serfs or slaves, so let us walk with the dignity (not arrogance) of those who call Him Father. We are not to be embarrassed because we own His Name; He is not ashamed of us, why should we be ashamed of Him?

Here is another promise God makes to us. We have seen that we are God's sons, but Romans 8:14–17 tells us that within us is the very spirit of sonship which enables us to call upon our Father in an intimate way – Abba. It goes on to talk about what happens when someone dies and the will is read. An heir is a person who receives a portion of an estate but we are called co-heirs. The difference between the two is that co-heirs inherit together all the estate.

Now Christ, the mediator of the New Covenant, died, which meant that all Christians are the inheritors of the kingdom of God together. What it means for us today is that as we walk as sons of God, we walk, live and act as possessors of His kingdom. Right now, we have all the resources to fulfil our commission. No Christian has more, or is better equipped, than any other. We are truly brothers and sisters in our service and loyalty.

2. *Let us live in the spirit of sonship.*
St Paul exhorts us to have a right attitude in heart and mind. We may not realise it but living any other way could be dishonouring to God. Too often, our emotions override the truth; a history of failure and despair, we feel, dictates our placement as second-class citizens in His kingdom. I have heard some say that you cannot be a son unless you always overcome. What nonsense! We must allow His Spirit to continually assure us that whether we succeed or fail at any task, we are for ever His sons – nothing can change that!

Learning to live in the spirit of sonship will mean making mistakes. Listen! Making a mistake is not a sin! It is part of the process of growing up. If you are not making the occasional mistake, then I wonder if you are learning to live in the spirit of sonship.

Have you ever watched a mother encouraging her child to walk? Hesitantly, he grips hold of the table leg, and when he is steady, he commences to wobble rather than walk across the floor. Suddenly, his tiny legs give way and he flops to the floor. Does his mother rush over to him and scold him severely for failing? Never! The mother is delighted; her child has taken some steps – quite unaided. No, a mistake is not a sin. We may sin when we refuse to learn from our mistakes.

Don't be afraid to experiment when necessary. Don't be afraid to make a mistake when learning to walk in the Spirit.

3. Let us delight in our fellowship with God.

Inga had never known how to delight in fellowship with God; she had never known the love of her father. She was one of the countless casualties of the Second World War who had been driven from one displaced persons' camp to another until, at last, she found refuge in England. She was a gentle soul and her simple faith had sustained her through trials and difficulties that had separated her from her family and friends, and from the land she had loved.

When she came to our community home at Longmead in Dorset, to one of the many seminars conducted by the Sacred Dance Group, we met a person who was sensitive, and if a little retiring, ever anxious to please. We loved her. It was during one of the workshops conducted by Paula Douthett, the director of the Sacred Dance Group, that a very moving incident occurred.

Paula had explained with great gentleness and understanding the truth that God is our Father, and that His desire is to draw us into the warm fellowship of His loving heart. To help bring home this truth she asked each person to sit on one chair with an empty chair beside them. 'Now,' she said, 'close your eyes and rest. When you are ready, invite your heavenly Father to come and sit by you. Allow Him to minister His life and love to your needs. Later, we will share our experiences.'

When the time came, many shared what they felt God had done and said to them, but none was so moving and meaningful as Inga's account.

She told of her unhappy experiences in Europe, of her loneliness and separation from her loved ones, and especially of how she had never known the love of a father. She continued, 'I did as I was told and placed a chair at my side. I sat there a while wondering what I should do next. I tried to imagine God as my father sitting by me but it wasn't very easy because I didn't know what to expect. What did a father do when he sat by you? I waited some more, then I thought that I would talk to him.

"Father!" I said, "do you mind me sitting by you?"

"No," He seemed to say, "I am so glad that you are sitting by my side."

I waited a while wondering what to say next. I was certainly no longer a child; I was a grown woman and not very elegant at that. How could He love me? But I risked going on.

"Father, please may I sit on your lap?"

"Yes, Inga," He said, "I'd like that very much."

So I moved over and sat on His chair imagining myself on His lap. He seemed to place His arms around me and I felt so warm. Then it occurred to me that I was a big woman and I wondered if I was too heavy.

"Am I too heavy for you, Father?" I asked.

"No, dear Inga," He said, "you're not at all heavy."

After a while longer, I said to Him, "Have I been here too long?"

"No, my dear," He replied, "stay as long as you like. I love having you in my arms." '

Her face was radiating such profound happiness as she said, 'So I snuggled down into His arms and He loved me in the most wonderful way that I have ever known.'

Inga had discovered the true meaning of fellowship with God. She was really part of His family, accepted in the beloved. She was no longer a wanderer, a reject and an oddity, but a very special person – to God Himself. God, her Father, delighted in Inga (and in all of us) coming as often as she could to find a place of solace in

His arms. If only we could learn from Inga the meaning of true fellowship with our Father.

An exercise in awareness and response.

To provide a practical edge to what we have been sharing I would like to suggest a small exercise which has often helped me to become more aware of our Father's nearness and relationship with us. Personally, I find it convenient to work in stages, my thinking works better that way. The mechanics are quite simple. We give our minds the pleasure of appreciating what we receive through the natural senses. This awakens in our spirits a response which usually takes the form of earnest prayer to our Father who is communing with us. Normally, I try to be alone but it can be as I am looking out of the window of a train, or driving the car, or simply walking to the bus stop. When I can I speak aloud or whisper what I'm thinking. I find this stops my thoughts from wandering.

For an example, let me recall a spring morning when I was standing at the front door of the house where I live. It was a beautiful, warm day; a bonus after a hard winter. My thinking and talking ran something like this.

(i) *'I'm really God's son.'* 'That's what I am . . . I really am one of God's millions of sons. I have millions of brothers and sisters . . . and yet, I'm special to Him. Amazing that, for I really can't see much in myself. I'm too ordinary to notice in a crowd . . . but what my Father says is what really matters. He loves me . . . and what is more, I know He loves me just as I am. That's remarkable too when I think of it.

'Lord, there must be so many who don't know you like this. Please hear their cries this beautiful morning! Shine on them just as this warm sunshine is shining on me now. You know, Lord, there's one thing about which

I'm certain, and that is, if there is a way to their hearts, you'll find it. Thank you for that, Lord!'

(ii) *'You are my Father, Lord.'* 'I still can't grasp this truth! The Lord Most High God is not simply my creator . . . but He's my Father! I need a new, expanded mind to take this in . . . but it's absolutely true! I'm standing here looking on all this beauty, and I can say that my Father made it. You can hear these very thoughts, can't you, Lord? I wonder how many millions of people have no idea what it is to have an ordinary father, let alone a heavenly Father? That's a frightening thought. There must be so much misery and loneliness in the world.

'Father, right now, I reach out my hands over this unhappy world and ask you to pour upon it as much healing and blessing as it can receive. There is so much fear and torment which is the product of man's greed and craze for power. Our Father, please hold in your great arms of love those who yearn for your righteousness, especially the children who have no one to turn to. Right now, dear Father, breathe into them your warm comfort and healing.'

(iii) *'You made all this, Father.'* 'Yes, everything that I can see has been made by my Father. You made it! That wonderful flowering cherry tree about to burst forth into a haze of pink. Those hedgerows . . . I still don't know their many names . . . not that it matters . . . they're still beautiful. And the grass itself . . . do you know Lord, I really believe it likes being walked on . . . it feels so good underfoot. And what about the countless smaller plants? . . . each is quite different, and in its own peculiar way, spectacular. Just think, our Father made all this . . . for us – His children! How blue is the sky today . . . how warm is the sun! You know, Father, your birds can't stop singing on a day like this, can they? You made them too . . . But isn't it sad to consider that our Father has given to us a world full of treasures and we spend our time destroying them?

'Lord, Father, we are such stupid and careless people. It's not that we don't know that we're destroying your precious gifts to us . . . we do! Forgive us, Father, and give to all of us who live on this wonderful earth a determination and energy to put an end to the havoc we're causing. Give to us caring hearts and a genuine will to bring to all things and to all men everywhere your peace and wholeness.'

(iv) *'You speak through what you've made.'* 'I've been so busy looking at everything around me, that I've not seen what is right at my feet . . . daffodils! Oh, magnificent! Do you remember last year when I used to say good morning to you? Well . . . good morning to you now! You lovely creatures of the soil . . . a host of beautiful faces looking at me . . . almost following me around. Thank you for your friendship! . . . you are so disarming. Do you know I can see in your lovely faces the face of our Creator? I've always thought of His beauty as something far beyond my appreciation . . . much too high for my poor spirit to reach. But this isn't so, is it? You . . . dear, dear Father, you are speaking to me through the faces of these daffodils. You are actually telling me of your love and care for me. Too soon they will fade and I will not see them again for another long year. But you have promised that you'll come again, haven't you, Father? . . . through your Son, that is. I may not see the flowers after they have passed away . . . but I have their memory. I won't forget!

'Oh Father, I want to thank you from the depths of my heart for having spoken to me today. Even when I cannot see you you are ever near me. There are so many people who haven't this consolation and I bring them to you now. In your mercy, Father, will you speak to them today? They may not know that it's you at first, but if you open their eyes, as you opened mine to these daffodils, then just maybe, they'll hear your still small voice. I would like that, very much . . . and I thank you, gentlest of fathers.'

A special prayer.

And now, to those of you who find it difficult, and even painful, to think of God as your Father may I suggest a prayer like this.

Dear Lord, I want to call you Father, but at present, I am having problems. From what the Scriptures say I know in my mind that you love me and that you have made me your son through Jesus Christ. However, I cannot feel this Father-love of yours at the moment. Please help me. May I call you my Friend?

Please teach me how to know you better, your plans for this world in which I live, and your longing for all mankind to honour you as Lord. Give to me listening ears, an understanding mind, and a compassionate heart, so that I may do only those things that please you.

As my love grows for you, I am certain that, one day, you, my dear Friend, will become my Father. I give you my thanks for all you have done for me, and for all you are going to do, in Jesus' Name. Amen.

8: Our Faithful Friend.

It was at the close of a Sunday service and I was saying goodbye to the people when a lady, with a rather determined look on her face, came and stood in front of me, and without any preamble, said, 'That was a good sermon, but what you need is the Holy Spirit! It would make all the difference.'

I was really piqued. Who was she to say that I needed the Holy Spirit – whatever she meant by it? That evening, I thought a great deal about what she had said, and after much painful self-examination, I came to realise that she was absolutely right. I really did need something more than I had, and that something more, I discovered later, was the third person of the Trinity – the Holy Spirit. But it presented me with a big question. My training told me that every Christian had the Holy Spirit, and so, how could I need more of Him, what should I expect, and how would He identify Himself? Perhaps you have been asking similar questions.

In this chapter we shall not be looking so much at the theology of the Holy Spirit but, rather, the activity and benefits of His presence in our lives. I am not a dogmatist but I see His work reaching far beyond the boundaries imposed by some earnest Christians.

Let us start with the promise of the Holy Spirit.

The promise.

When Jesus said goodbye to His close disciples, He left them with a promise that He would send to them the

Holy Spirit who would be their friend, counsellor, comforter, guide, teacher, advocate, in fact, everything He had been to them. He would not leave them alone and friendless.

This promise was fulfilled on the Day of Pentecost when the Spirit came in a rush of mighty wind filling all who were gathered in an upper room in Jerusalem (Acts 2:1–4). St Peter explained who the promise was for in his first Spirit-charged sermon. 'For the promise is to you, and to your children, and to all that are afar off', and adding, as if some should see this as a promise to Israel only, 'and to everyone whom the Lord our God calls to him' (Acts 2:39). Now that includes all the Gentiles from every country of the world and from every age – if they have called on His Name.

Regarding the beneficiaries of the promise, I do not think anything could be clearer. Two facts are certain.

1. The Holy Spirit has come.
2. He is residing in the Church of Christ.

Surely, the Church of Christ is made up of Christians – the good, the not so good, the clever, the less clever, every sort you can think of. It is a unity (Eph. 4:15–16). Now, if the Church is truly Christ's body, then I do not see how He can be resident in just parts of it. The Holy Spirit is the life of the body, and the head of this body is Christ.

I don't think that we will go far wrong if we keep these basic truths before us. What we shall consider in this chapter is the effect of His presence, what He is to us, and what we mean by receiving Him.

The effect of His presence.

It is certainly difficult to describe the effect of His presence because, usually, He is so gentle, almost subtle, in His dealings with us. We know that He is the personal presence of Jesus and that without Him we cannot function or live as Christians. Perhaps I can liken it to an experience I enjoyed in Zimbabwe.

Some years ago, I visited the beautiful town of Umtali. It was jacaranda time, and as I came through the high pass and looked down on the town I saw the great splashes of purple, red and white that mingled with the gracious buildings and the green of the parks and gardens. It was such a contrast after the long drive through dry countryside from the capital, Harare, that I left the car by the roadside and found a place to sit down. I was perspiring and longed for a cool drink, but I longed even more to spend a few minutes gazing on this jewel of a town which lay in a near-circle of undulating hills. 'A truly wonderful sight,' I said to myself, but then added, 'but there's something missing and I can't make out what it is.'

Then, something happened which transformed the whole scene for me. It was a natural occurrence and it didn't, in fact, change what I saw. What it did was to affect me in such a delightful way that my appreciation of the scene was transformed.

A most cooling and refreshing wind blew through the pass. That was all.

I remember to this day how invigorated I felt as I travelled down into Umtali. Just a simple wind – but it blew, for me, at the right place and at the right time.

No wonder the people of God in the Bible used such symbols as water, wind, oil and wine to speak of the Holy Spirit. They would have a special meaning. Water and rain were vital ingredients for a happy and productive existence; the cool breeze of the evening after a hot day made the time of rest pleasant and enjoyable, and oil and wine were for celebration as well as healing. All these were gifts from a good God, and the abundance of them meant, not only well-being and prosperity, but especially that He had seen fit to dwell in their company.

It is difficult to describe the effect of the Spirit in our

lives. He is indeed like water, wind, oil and wine to us twenty-four hours a day, but as we grow in sensitivity and discernment, we shall notice too those special high moments when we shall say, 'Yes, that was the gentle wind of the Spirit,' or 'That was the wine of His joyful presence!'

The difference between 'with' and 'in'.

We may be fully convinced that the Holy Spirit is with us, but He is wanting a relationship that is the closest possible. John 14:17 describes it as an 'in' relationship – as distinct from 'with'.

Perhaps, right now, some of us are lacking the joy and excitement of Christian living, our sight has grown dim because we have resorted to planning our own future. We long for His water to quench our thirst, His warmth to encourage us, a rekindled zeal in our fight against the enemy. We cry out for this 'in' experience with God. We feel more like guests than sons, and there is a great difference.

Let us say you invite a person to join your family. He may come as a guest or as a member. A guest, while he may be treated with respect and even love, remains a guest. He knows what he is allowed to do and what he must not do, and that barrier remains between himself and the family.

How different it is when a person is allowed to become an actual member of the family. Every door is opened to him so that he is able to enjoy a status and an intimacy equal to every other member. This intimacy the Holy Spirit desires to have with us. We declare that we belong to Him yet how much of us is truly surrendered to Him? Jesus said, 'If a man loves me, he will keep my word, and my Father will love him, and we will come to him and make our home with him' (John 14:23). Asking God to take that in-place in our hearts and lives is an act of will. We willingly give ourselves to receive Him fully into our lives – no longer guests but sons – but even more, we willingly co-operate with whatever He wants to do in and through us. So, this is not just surrender but joyful participation, actively using the gifts He gives to us.

What then, is the activity of the Holy Spirit in us?

The work of the Holy Spirit.

If I am thirsty and I drink a glass of fresh, cool water, the immediate effect is one of satisfaction and refreshment. But, of course, it does not stop there. The water passes into my system to assist my bodily functions, which in turn, helps me live a little more fully.

When the Spirit of the Lord is granted the freedom to move freely in our lives we may experience many remarkable effects, but these effects are produced as a result of the work He is doing in us. You could say that the 'freeing medium' that enables the Spirit to move efficiently is love. The more we love God and one another, the more active the Spirit is, and the more Jesus is seen to live in us. It's as simple as that.

We may learn a great deal about the work of the Holy Spirit from chapters fourteen to sixteen of the Gospel of St John. This is the account of the talk that Jesus had with His disciples at the Last Supper. Jesus described Him as their comforter and counsellor, as one who would stand by them to guide and help them in times of trouble. He would be their closest friend.

What did Jesus say of the Holy Spirit? How does this special encouragement to his disciples influence us today?

1. He is the Spirit of truth.
John 14:15–16 tells us that if we love Jesus and keep His commandments, then the Holy Spirit will be to us the Spirit of truth. We live in a world fraught with difficulties and dangers; a world in which it is often a

problem to distinguish between right and wrong, good and evil, darkness and light. There are so many opinions and points of view that to walk God's way with any real certainty is sometimes near to impossible. This is where we need our special Counsellor, the Holy Spirit. Every moment of the day and night He is with us gently interpreting all the events, both great and small, in the light of truth. He gives to us that warm assurance so that we don't have to stumble into error or deceit. However, let us always keep in mind that God works best in an environment of love. Love and truth walk hand in hand.

2. *He is our teacher and remembrancer.*
To grow in the life of the Spirit there are things to learn, and learning is a process – it takes time. To learn anything well requires a good teacher. This the Holy Spirit has promised to be, and He does His job well. It can mean putting aside preconceived ideas and permitting Him to lay an entirely new foundation; then He commences to build, precept upon precept, line upon line (Isa. 28:10), until our knowledge is more strong and sure.

3. *He is a witness to Jesus.*
As I have already mentioned, the sole work of the Holy Spirit is to make Jesus a reality. John 15:26–27 emphasises that He is the Spirit of truth, and therefore, this testimony of His is a truthful one. It takes courage to talk about Jesus to others but He has a remarkable way of putting the right words into our mouths, so, try not to be afraid. The people we talk to may be more anxious than you think to hear what we have to say. If we try to be faithful we may be sure that He will be faithful to us.

4. *He announces things to come.*
John 16:13 assures us that the future is in God's hands. There is nothing left to chance in the planning of our

lives. He wants us to be intelligent participators in all
that he does here on earth, so that as we look ahead, we
are filled with hope. Time, as we know it, is for the sake
of moral order, and the Spirit of God lives and acts
outside these restrictions. He is eternal, and although we
are citizens of an eternal kingdom, at present our human
and finite minds can cope with only so much revelation.
This is why He sometimes speaks to us in parables,
types, allegories, shadows etc. Nevertheless, I believe
that He can reveal wonderful truths at times concerning
the future and He would have us to be as receptive as
possible.

5. He will be Jesus to us.

Almost two thousand years have passed away and still
the testimony of Jesus remains sure and firm in the hearts
of those who believe on Him. Our faith does not rest on
the accuracy of historical evidence but in the truth that
He is alive in His Church. All that He was to his disciples
He can be to us; He hasn't changed.

When Jesus appeared to Thomas, after he had
doubted His resurrection, He said to him, 'Have you
believed because you have seen me?' and went on,
'Blessed are those who have not seen yet believe.' We
have not seen, but we believe, and we are able to believe
because the resurrected Christ lives within us by the
power of the Holy Spirit. His ministry is to make Jesus
real to us for He is still the friend of sinners, the healer
of the broken, the companion of the lonely, the
comforter of the frightened, the sustainer of the weary.

Yes, it is a good thing to give thanks to God for his
mercy.

What do we mean by receiving the Holy Spirit?

Those many people who gave themselves to writing the
many books of the Bible were not thinking in terms of
a theological treatise or even an historical record, but

rather, an account of God's redemptive purpose towards man and His dealings with them through the centuries. The Israelites, in particular, were very poetic and descriptive in their form of communication. They freely used figures, types and symbols to add impact and meaningfulness to their message.

And so it was that when the writers of the New Testament related the story of the promises and coming of the Holy Spirit they spoke of Him as rivers of living water flowing out of the heart (John 7:38), of being baptised (Acts 1:5), or as not yet fallen (Acts 8:16). This was quite natural, and they were speaking about the one and same experience – receiving the Spirit as promised by Jesus.

Today, we hear of Christians talking about 'being baptised in the Spirit', or 'being filled with the Spirit', or occasionally 'being imbued with power.' Really the expression employed doesn't matter so long as we understand it to mean what Jesus meant.

The early Christians were mainly Jews who tried to describe this remarkable phenomenon in the most graphic and communicable way possible. Some felt it was like an abundance of life-giving water flowing through them, others, as if they were being plunged into the pool of life, and there were those who described it as a gentle refreshing rain falling on them. But all received the same promised Holy Spirit.

The moment of receiving.

Can we be sure of the moment we receive the Spirit? I suppose it depends on what we mean by receiving. I know of some people who exercise clear spiritual gifts without ever having asked for a special baptism; they grew in the knowledge of the use of them. I know of others who have themselves prayed, or have received prayer, and some have then exercised spiritual gifts and some have not. But there are a few I have met who said something like this. 'I recalled the day when I was confirmed. The bishop laid his hands on me and prayed that I would receive the Holy Spirit. Nothing seemed to happen and I forgot about it. Much later, I realised what had happened and I told myself that I should enter into what had been promised me – and I've been using certain of the gifts ever since.'

I think that there is the secret – expectancy and acceptance.

If a good friend knocked on the door of your home, what would you do? Why, you would open the door, greet him, and ask him to come inside and make him welcome. I don't think you would open the door, greet him, and then close the door in case he decided not to come in. That would be unnatural and rude. Galatians 3:14 says that we receive the promise of the Spirit through faith. Let me tell you of the assurance I received.

Faith and works.

It was a month after I had made my confirming prayer for this baptism of filling with the Holy Spirit and I was still desperate. I felt just as I was before. Even the evidence of that special night I doubted and I wondered where I had gone wrong. It's remarkable the advice you receive from so many well-meaning folk at such a time.

And so, one Saturday night four weeks later, I determined to open my heart to God. I asked myself whether I was seeking some new sensation or spiritual euphoria. I could honestly say no to that question. As I thought about it more it became clear that what I really wanted was something that would last. I wanted the Bible to unfold the great mysteries of God; it was so stuffy as it was. I wanted a vital and productive prayer life; I hoped that wasn't asking too much. And one more thing, I wanted to be relaxed about talking to others about my faith.

I knelt by my bed quite alone. What would the

outcome be? Well, one thing was sure, I would receive nothing unless I expected it, and I was going to expect God to answer my prayer that night. This was the sort of prayer I prayed.

'If I have actually received your promise, then I reverently ask you to do three things. Firstly, when I open my Bible to read it, I want it to come alive to my imagination and heart. I want it to help me live. Secondly, when I come to you in prayer and worship you, I want you to let me know that you really are present. Let me know your love filling my heart. And thirdly, Lord, when tomorrow comes, will you give me the opportunity to help someone? Please give me the necessary courage and freedom. Thank you so much, Lord. From this moment I'm going to expect it to happen. Amen.'

This prayer was not a prayer telling God what to do, but one in which I told myself what He was promising. I was wanting to honour His integrity.

Rather nervously, I opened my Bible and looked at the passage in St John's Gospel about the shepherd and his sheep. I said to myself, 'Right, here goes!' Never before had this message become so startlingly clear. It was rather like meeting the shepherd and learning from him first-hand. I conditioned myself to expect, and I received. When I prayed that night it was no longer me speaking to someone in the far distance. God seemed so much nearer, like talking to a close friend. I began to understand the meaning of communion. It was the most thrilling discovery I had made in years. The next day, I was full of anticipation, really wanting to talk and help some needy person. I didn't want to be a bore. Well, I was not disappointed. God showed me an elderly man and I was able to talk to him in a very low-key way about one or two of his problems. I was delighted and so grateful.

Yes, this was the Holy Spirit at work – in a new way, after so many years. Do be encouraged.

A group exercise.

It is difficult to understand the truth that the Holy Spirit can be at work in us all at the same time, but it is a fact. Although, temperamentally and characteristically. we are so different, yet the more our love-relationship develops, the more we shall discern this common mind of Christ by the Spirit. In today's language we might say that 'we'll be on the same wavelength'.

This group exercise will highlight the truths that each of us has a valid, special contribution to make to the whole, and that this whole has the mark of the person who makes it possible – the Holy Spirit.

The group is going to create a psalm together. Any number of people may participate, and arranging the chairs in the form of a circle is best, it brings us a little closer to each other. The leader will then explain the details of the exercise. Perhaps it will be something like this.

'God is going to show us just how creative we are. Have you ever written a poem or a song, or even painted a picture? Very few of us have, and so wrongly we draw the conclusion that we are not creative types, not easily inspired. Well, that may be true in one sense, but it is not true when we invite the Holy Spirit to help us. As we learn how to allow Him to move in us, either individually or corporately, we learn how to distinguish His person and closeness. It doesn't take long to understand that someone is with us, helping us. This exercise will do this.

'Now a psalm is a song, and usually when we talk about psalms we immediately think of the Book of Psalms in the Bible. This is quite natural; we are reasonably familiar with their patterns, and we may use these patterns for our psalm.

'We say that the Book of Psalms is inspired and it will be the same Holy Spirit who will inspire us now. But, you know, it's difficult to discern what we mean by inspired. We could say that it is anything that inspires. Read one of the Psalms, and then ask ourselves, how did the Holy Spirit speak to us, what exactly did he say? We can't put our finger on it, but we certainly felt much better afterwards, as though we had received something tangible from someone very special. This is what we may experience as we share in the making of our psalm.

'All right, what do we do? First of all we need someone to be our scribe; preferably, someone who can write clearly and reasonably fast. Then I want us all to relax and really enjoy our exercise. It will be helpful if we all close our eyes and I will guide you through. May I suggest that we write a fifteen-line psalm – it can be more or less, it doesn't matter. All you contribute is just one line and you may share in any order you wish. And please, there is no such thing as a mistake! No doubt when you have shared a line you will think to yourself afterwards, "That was terrible!" I want to tell you now that it wasn't. Wait until the end and all will be revealed. You will see then how important your contribution was.

'This is how I will guide you.

1. First, we offer a prayer asking for the Holy Spirit's encouragement.

2. Then, I will offer the first line of our psalm. I will repeat it so that our scribe can take it down. I will be in contact with her all the time so that you may keep your eyes closed.

3. When she is ready, I will say, "Next please". Then, in any order, you may make your single-line contribution. I will repeat that line so that everyone may hear it. When our scribe has that line down, I will say again, "Next please".

4. And so we continue until we have composed all fifteen lines.

'Do keep in mind that you may be as flexible as you wish. You may extend somebody else's line, if you wish, but do be yourselves. If half way through you feel a "Praise the Lord" or a "Hallelujah" is appropriate, then don't think it out of place.'

Here is an example of a psalm we produced at a parish weekend. This was a middle-of-the-road Anglican church with a wide age range, and we shared in this exercise about two days into the conference. It was a totally new experience for them.

We rejoice in your presence, O Lord our king.
We sing your praises with glad hearts.
We come before you with tambourines, dancing in your presence,
Your love and peace are always overflowing.
Lord, let our souls burst with the beauty of your holiness and your peace.
Come to our inner hearts.
You are our life-line, and we bow in adoration,
For you are the glory, and the power.
Hallelujah!
Your kingdom is everlasting
Your ways are ever sure, and your understanding never fails.
Without you we are nothing!
Your power is all that is needed.
We magnify your holy Name.
Praise you, Lord!
We love you, Lord!
Hallelujah!'

Just a word to the leader. Try to be sensitive to what God is doing and the difficulties some may be having. Occasionally, you may have to encourage in order to maintain the flow so that the previous contribution will be kept before them. At the beginning you may offer another line yourself or give the others a further opportunity, but once they are relaxed, you might find it a little difficult to hold them. It can be a very exciting time.

To close the exercise, you may find it helpful if any would care to share their experiences. You could ask questions like these. Did you notice the part your contribution made to the whole? Did you notice the theme? It was rather like being on the same wavelength, wasn't it? Did you notice the gentle manner in which the Holy Spirit was in control when we agreed to do this exercise together? How would you describe His presence in you, personally? Have you noticed Him working in similar ways in your life before? Did you observe that in no way did He take from you the right to choose?

Many interesting discussions may follow.

We need the rain.

I remember one year at Longmead we sowed a few packets of seeds in the seedframes. When we came to plant them out in the garden the ground was dryish which meant that we had to resort to the watering can. They grew very slowly and we thought they would produce only a few flowers. Somehow, I could never provide them with enough water – until the showers of rain came. Almost miraculously they grew into large blossoming plants, and that year, we had a garden that was a blaze of colour.

You see, there was residual water in the ground and there was added water from the watering can, but it was the showers of rain that did the trick.

The early Church needed the rain of the Holy Spirit, and so do we. We must stop praying for the Holy Spirit to come – He has come! He has come to empower all God's people, but more than that, He has come to bind us together and fashion us into one body – called the Church (Eph. 2:5–6, 1 Cor. 12:13–27, Acts 2:47).

Yes, He has come, so let us joyfully receive Him! Let us take down our umbrellas of doubt and unbelief!

Here is a prayer to help any who desire to receive the Spirit's indwelling now.

Gracious Father, as one of your children I recognise my great need of your Holy Spirit. The Bible tells me that He is with me, but I desire so much for Him to take full possession of my life. I want to be more than a passive believer; I want to be an active participator.

Please purify me from all sin and self-centredness, so that I may be a temple fit for Him to live in.

Right now, Lord, as I bow before you, I open to you the door of my will. Come in and possess me. I humbly receive you! I joyfully receive you! Direct my heart, my mind and thinking, my faculties and senses, my hopes and aspirations, so that Jesus may be seen living and reigning in me. Thank you, Lord! I believe and receive! Amen.

9: A Living Faith.

Faith is not the easiest of truths to understand. We talk of having it, or not too much of it, but we are never quite sure what we mean. Then, to talk of faith in God, a person we cannot even see, presents more problems.

I am going to suggest that we try to understand faith in God by examining the faith we have for day-to-day living. In fact, the principles are the same. Let us begin by using an example of a person who died after what many of her friends believed to be the prayer of faith. It raises certain important questions.

Lord, why did you allow it to happen?

'Denis, is that you?' came the despairing voice over the telephone. 'Maggie's dead!' There was a long pause; I wanted her to have time to think. 'And Denis,' she went on slowly labouring each word, 'I'm completely shattered . . . and my faith in a loving God is at an all-time low . . . Why did God allow this to happen?'

I stood looking at the mouthpiece of the telephone not knowing how to answer in her present state of shock. I had heard about Maggie through Julie who was now speaking to me. I knew from conversations at a conference that she was an active member of a parish church prayer group in Sussex. She had delighted in telling me the remarkable answers to prayer they had received.

'Julie,' I said, 'do please tell me what has happened.' She needed no further encouragement.

'Well, you know I've told you about our prayer group.

Through all the time we've been together we've discovered a close relationship with God. He's been so good to us. Maggie was part of the group, you know. We loved her . . . I think everyone in the church did. She was always helping folk here, and we felt that if anyone knew God it was her.

'Two months ago, Maggie had to go to hospital for a check-up – she had pains in her chest. Naturally, we all prayed for her. Later, we received the terrible news that she had cancer. I can tell you, Denis, we were shocked . . . we all were. That Sunday Ken, our vicar, asked the whole church to pray. Then a week ago she had to go into hospital; she was getting worse and worse and in great pain. Ken called for a night of prayer and fasting. I think the whole church must have turned out. You'll never believe how hard we prayed! There were also many tears shed because she was loved so much.

'Then, about three in the morning, a number of us had words we believe were from God that He was going to heal her; it was not a sickness unto death. You can imagine our joy! Maggie was going to be made better! When Maggie was told she was thrilled too – naturally. And do you know, Denis, from that moment we began to see definite signs of improvement. When I went to visit her she was sitting up in bed. What a relief it was!'

There was another long pause as Julie tried to muster her thoughts to share what had followed. Gently, I encouraged her to continue.

'Yesterday, I phoned the hospital to find out how she was, and to get some idea when they would let her come home . . . and they told me . . . that she'd had a relapse . . . She's dead!'

Then poured out the bitter thoughts and questions that had plagued her since.

'Denis, why? . . . Why did God allow such a dreadful thing to happen? We were so sure He'd heal her! We've had such faith to believe that it was His will . . . but now . . . some of us are so stunned and shattered that it'll be a long time before we're able to pray properly again.'

Some important questions.

How distressing and perplexing an experience like that can be. What could have gone wrong? Initial reaction questions whether God is really a God of love. Does He really raise our hopes to dash them to the ground, or is He a God who makes promises only to break them to see how we stand up to the trials and tribulations of life? In saner moments we know that this cannot be. Naturally, we require time to sort out our thoughts and feelings, and then, perhaps, we ask ourselves questions like, were the words that were purported to have come from God actually from Him? Could they have been prompted from a longing to have our prayers answered, or, when we felt faith rising within us, was it in fact faith, or simply a warm sense of agreement which emerged from a time of close fellowship and prayer?

Difficult questions to answer. Perhaps if we could have a better appreciation of the 'mechanics' of faith, and what faith is, more light will shine in our darkness.

For some time I questioned whether I truly understood what was meant by faith. It is easy to say that we have it when there is a rise in what appears to be 'confidence' – confidence that God is going to answer a prayer. But why are so many of these prayers not answered? I quite realise that we say that God answers in His own inexplicable way, but frankly, I'm not very convinced by that explanation. When the early followers of Jesus prayed they received what they asked for, and I think we should receive more than we do. So, we are going to look at faith and see if we can find some answers to the questions that may puzzle us.

What the Bible says faith is.

The most illustrative and definitive Scripture on faith is found in Hebrews 11:1. It says that faith is two things:

1. The assurance of things hoped for, and
2. The conviction of things not seen.

The rephrased verse may read that, 'faith is the assurance and conviction of things we hope for but are not yet seen.'

You could say that the word 'assurance' is something which has actual existence; it has substance, or real being. 'Conviction' can also be translated 'evidence.'

Let us imagine we are digging in the garden, the fork hits something hard and there is the sound of breaking. We clear away the immediate soil and there is a piece of old pottery. At first it does not look much to shout about but we ask an expert just in case it is. He examines the piece of pottery and assures us that it could be an important find. In a moment of time, a pot we cannot see, because it is hidden in the ground as yet, becomes something we 'confidently expect' to find when we do dig it up. (May I point out that the word 'hope' means to 'confidently expect'.) Now the reason we confidently expect to find the pot in the ground, which at present we cannot see, is because we hold in our hands a piece of its substance. We may observe the formation of the lip but there is a jagged edge as well. This substance is evidence. There can be no doubt whatsoever.

What we must bear in mind is that the piece of the pot, which is the substance and evidence, is not in itself the activity of digging up the remainder. This activity arises from a confident expectation to find it. You could say the order is: the piece of pottery, which is the substance and evidence of the pot hidden in the ground, because of its value has given rise to a confident expectation to find it if we dig for it.

Let me illustrate this truth another way. I am given a valid train ticket to London by a friend. It is only a piece of card and I can handle and read it. On it are printed details and conditions of the journey. This is substance and evidence (or assurance and conviction) that I can make the journey. To use this ticket I must have confident expectation that when I show it at the ticket barrier they will permit me to board the train. But confident expectation is not enough by itself. I must walk to the train and climb aboard it, and allow it to carry me to my destination.

Faith is rather like the piece of pottery, or the train ticket.

No faith without a promise.

We cannot really talk about 'faith in action' or 'active faith' unless we understand it to mean a faith that gives rise to confident expectation (hope) to act. This is why James 2:20 says that, 'faith apart from works is dead (or barren)'. The reason I have emphasised this is because we tend to mix up faith with our emotions. We may focus all our attention on believing we have faith, convinced that the emotional response is evidence of increased faith, which leads us to consider another important factor – promise.

You may have realised by now that we cannot talk of faith in the same way as a piece of pottery or as a train ticket because in fact, you cannot handle, see, or even quantify it. Of course, all illustrations and analogies have their limitations, and so do ours. How may we know then if we have real faith? We ask whether it is based on a promise. This way helps us to sort our faith from our feelings.

Think this through, if you will. You cannot have faith in a thing, or an experience, or anything at all – only in a promise made by a person or persons. Impossible! Well, let me explain.

A friend telephones to say that he will be calling to see me at, say, eleven o'clock on a Wednesday morning. I know him well enough to expect him at that time precisely. At a little before the time I set my work aside and prepare some coffee. He arrives as agreed, we drink our coffee and talk. My faith was conditioned by the promise he made, and confidently expecting him, I set my work aside and prepared the coffee for the occasion. You see, once the promise was made, there was 'something' in my thinking and consciousness that was almost substantial and very reassuring. It was the evidence and conviction I needed. I could not handle or see it, but it made me confidently expect him and act accordingly.

Faith and our emotions.

We begin to see that faith has nothing to do with our emotions although they often become mixed. Our problem is that it is so difficult to describe what faith is. It does not make any noise; it cannot be measured or contained, but we can be assured of it when we have it. We may even understand faith to be the legitimate grounds for hoping, and yet, it is more.

In every day life we are continually exercising faith in promises made by so many people, or groups of people, under all kinds of circumstances, so much so, that we hardly notice we are doing it. It is a natural part of survival. In our spiritual life too, we are exercising faith in the promises of our Lord, for the most part, without realising it. It is when we are confronted by some difficult situation or problem that we wonder just how much we have.

Allow me to share an experience showing how naturally we may receive God's blessings through faith.

Lord, this house is your property!

Not long after we moved into Longmead we encountered one of the worst winters in many years. The snowstorms were so heavy and numerous that we were cut off for five days. Unfortunately, this was the least of our worries. The loft area of Longmead is extensive, and because much of the roof is original, the spaces between the tiles allowed huge quantities of snow to enter. Ceilings threatened to collapse and we spent two days and much of the nights desperately removing the snow. It was a terrible time for as we cleared one part so another was being covered.

The following year I found myself dreading the coming winter but the New Year came and went with only a few flurries, until the first week in February.

I was working in the garden and it was frosty with a bright, clear blue sky. Surely, the promise of good things to come. Around ten-thirty, I decided to put away my tools and return to the house for a welcome cup of tea. I opened the door to let myself in when I happened to cast my eyes back. What I saw made my heart sink. The sky to the north was completely filled with heavy grey snow clouds – and they were approaching fast. In a matter of minutes the clouds were overhead and heavy showers of swirling snow were descending covering everything with a white mantle. The garage doors swung wildly to and fro threatening to break away from the hinges. I had to act swiftly.

I threw open the door of the house and rushed in to fetch a pair of Wellington boots. As I slipped on the second boot I stopped absolutely still. 'Oh Lord, the roof!' I cried, 'the loft area must be filling with fine snow!' Then it dawned, this was God's house. We had formed a charitable trust insisting that there should no personal shares in it. It would be His for all time, at least, as long as we lived. At that moment a strange calm came over me. I looked upwards and said this prayer to the Lord. 'Lord, with respect, what are you doing? You are able to look after your own property, and this is yours, isn't it?'

Not a cloud in the sky.

I felt so happy and lighthearted as I went outside to close the garage doors, and what I saw filled me with astonishment. I simply couldn't believe my eyes! The snow was on the ground but there was no wind at all, and there was not a trace of cloud anywhere to be seen in the sky. The sun shone and the sky was the bluest of blues. I still couldn't take it in so I climbed to the top of a nearby hill and gazed around me in sheer wonder. There wasn't even a slight haze let alone a cloud. I went back to the house and climbed into the loft to see the damage there, but there was not a snowflake to be seen anywhere – not even a patch of damp! How could I explain it?

Don't you think that so often the more natural we are with God, the more able we are to believe? We spend so much time trying to believe when, in fact, believing should be as natural as breathing.

One more point: I realise now that faith requires no specially formulated prayer, although they can be helpful. When I prayed that prayer I did not mean to be impertinent. In retrospect, what I think I was saying in that time of stress was, 'Denis, you idiot, don't you appreciate that this house is God's. Hasn't He promised to look after it, so get out of the way!' And I did.

Look for the conditions.

In most legal documents there are what are called provisos or conditions. Sometimes we regard them as the small print of the document because they appear to be conditions written in small print in order to trap the unwary . . . Perhaps in some instances this is true but nothing can change the fact that they are as important as the parts which enumerate the benefits. Too many well-meaning people have found themselves in difficulties because they have not taken enough trouble to read and understand the conditions of a contract. All promises, whether written or verbal, may or may not have conditions.

Here is an everyday example of a verbal promise with a condition.

If the 172 bus is running!

A conversation similar to this is not uncommon.

'Bill, could you meet me at the station at eight tonight? There are one or two things I'd like to talk over with you.'

'That'd be great, John. Oh, just one thing, my car's out of action and I'll have to come by bus . . . that's if the 172 is running.'

'Do that, Bill! Be seeing you then. Goodbye.'

'Goodbye, John.'

Bill has made John a promise to meet him at the station at eight o'clock that evening. However there is a condition. It is if the 172 bus is running. If Bill should not turn up on time for any other reason, then he has broken his promise, but if Bill should not turn up at the station at eight o'clock because the 172 bus had failed to arrive, then John will have considered him to have kept his promise within the terms of the agreement.

I know it may seem as if I am stating the obvious but it is so important.

God's conditions.

Now all the information that John and Bill needed to know concerning the promise and conditions was contained in their conversation. When we consider the promises in Scripture we have to take special care in reading any promise in the context of the whole Bible, at least, from a particular Book in the Bible. Here is an example from St John's Gospel.

132

The first promise is from John 14:13 and appears to be quite unconditional.

Whatever you ask in my Name, I will do it.

If that is so, then I could ask for a fine house, a Rolls Royce car, a villa in Italy, a cruiser on the Mediterranean, and so on. There are no limits to the 'whatever', are there? However, in the next chapter, John 15:7, we read

If you abide in me, and my words abide in you, ask whatever you will, and it shall be done for you.

Immediately our problem is solved. The conditions make it clear that only if I am abiding in Him and His words are abiding in me can I ask for whatever I will. It will mean that I will ask for only those things that are according to His perfect will.

Integrity – the value of a promise.

We know that a promise can be made only by a person and the value of that promise will depend on the integrity of the person. A definition of the word integrity is: 'adherence to moral principles' or 'honesty'. It is not long before we discover the integrity of a person. We shall discern it, in part, especially as we develop an appreciation for his consistency and genuineness in keeping his promises. If Bill keeps his promises nine out of ten times, then John may say to himself when he makes an appointment to meet him, 'I can rely on Bill, he rarely lets me down.' John's assurance (faith) rests on Bill's promise, and so he confidently expects the meeting will take place because he appreciates Bill's integrity.

Of course the best way to determine the integrity of a person is to get to know him. Let me tell you of Ralph. I think this will illustrate what I mean.

A man of integrity.

Ralph Dringer was the most eccentric man I had ever met. We met in the Army and worked together in Greece and Palestine teaching rather unwilling soldiers. Everything Ralph did was precise and very correct, and it was soon apparent that he was a stickler for honest dealings. Most of us were amused, particularly after seeing him one day, walking the black market district of Athens with a large board attached to his haversack on which was written, 'No black-marketing here, please! Thank you!' No one could really fathom the depths of Ralph for his lifestyle was not consistent with Army ways. What I found perplexing, however, was that I thoroughly enjoyed his company.

Ralph was different! What caused me later on to respect and honour this man, in spite of his eccentricities, was his love for God and his fellow human beings. Nothing could dissuade him from reaching out a helping hand to those less fortunate than himself. Often he would leave the camp in a borrowed jeep to take food supplies (honestly gained, I might add) to the poor in the villages around Athens. I came to realise that his odd ways were the means of hiding his charitable deeds. Many smiled at his peculiarities, but no one refused his friendship.

Had you asked me when I first met Ralph whether he was a man of integrity, I could not have given you a clear reply. Asked if he kept his promises, I would have replied, 'I think so.' But after months of living and woking with him, my answer to you would have been (and still is), 'I have never known a man of integrity like this man. I would trust him with my life', and I would have meant it.

And so we see that when a person keeps the promises he makes, he gradually reveals his integrity and honesty, but only when we experience his life and character firsthand can we be really sure.

Summary of essentials of faith.

Let us recap here the main truths of our discussion on faith.

1. Faith is the assurance and conviction of things hoped for but not yet seen.
2. There can be no faith apart from a promise made by someone.
3. Faith is not dependent on our emotions although they are often present.
4. A promise may or may not have accompanying conditions.
5. The value or dependency of any promise will rest on the integrity of the person making it.

The integrity of God.

How do we make faith a reality, or, how do we discover the integrity of God? The answer is simple. We must not only get to know about Him, we must get to know Him, or in other words, we must learn how to live with Him. The secret is dwelling in the Most Holy Place with Him. This is the reason for writing this book. Faith is for us the essential ingredient which makes it possible to receive and enjoy all that God has given to us. It is also the ingredient which enables us to be fully given to Him, consecrated, usable.

And without faith it is impossible to please him for whoever would draw near to him must believe that he exists and that he rewards those who seek him.
(Heb. 11:6)

A prayer for this closer relationship.

Lord, I long for a deeper understanding of the meaning of faith. I pray for such an assurance and conviction in your great promises so that I may confidently expect to receive anything you want me to have. In so doing, Lord, I honour you and cause those around me to see your Son, Jesus.

And Lord, please draw me closer to yourself so that I may daily know you as a friend who dwells within me; a friend who shares his life with me, and causes his love to be shed abroad through me. May our relationship grow in the bonds of perfect love so that I may be surrendered to your sovereign will. Then I will know how to walk by faith.

All this I desire that you might be glorified. Through Jesus Christ, my Saviour, I offer this prayer to you. Amen.

10: God's Gift That Brings Us Closer.

The name we give to this special gift is 'forgiveness'. It is the beautiful gift whereby God stimulates us to be so disposed in mind and heart that we may receive and offer freedom from any offences we may have committed against Him or against any other. The truth is that any kind of sin is a sin against God. It brings bondage of some kind or other and it mars our communion with God. Until we are released from it we cannot hope to enjoy a normal, happy life. What I find to be such a consolation is that no sin is too great for God to forgive, such is His love and desire for man to be restored to Him. The mark of true forgiveness is freedom and happiness.

Forgiveness that meant so much.

It was near the close of the evening service when Paul cautiously entered the church, found a seat, and sat there with his head bowed. He was not more than twenty-six years of age, poorly dressed, and appeared to be experiencing some form of inner turmoil. It was not uncommon for strangers to approach us for financial or material help, but as I looked into his sad face, I was certain that he was there for a more important reason.

Later, over a cup of tea, Paul told us with frankness the story of his life. He was married with two children and lived in Leeds. He had been in prison for various offences and as a result he had seen little of his family. He was, at present, on his way to London to join his friends to do a break-in job. The lift he had hitched had

137

brought him as far as our town, and experiencing a desperation to break free from what lay ahead of him, he had seen our church and had come in. He had no idea what to expect or whether any help would be forthcoming. He was there and that was it.

That night Paul came into a deep knowledge of God's forgiveness and love. He wanted to return home immediately and tell the good news to his wife who had known only abuse and separation from him. We urged him to stay the night so that when he returned it would be with a gift of money and clothes to help him begin his new life.

A week later, his wife wrote to us telling of the profound happiness they were enjoying. 'For the first time in fifteen years,' she said, 'Paul is decorating the house, and do you know what? – He's got a job! It's too wonderful to be true.' I keep that letter in my Bible as a treasure from the Lord. But the story does not end there.

Some months passed before she sent another letter which told of his death. She wrote, 'Such was the forgiveness that Paul had received from God, that he couldn't live knowing that there were still many unconfessed crimes he had committed. So he went to the local police station and told them everything. They were amazed! The judge said that because of what had happened to Paul he would send him away for only three months. When he was released one of the officers told me how he'd behaved. Every night, Paul would kneel down by his bed and pray. Everybody would laugh and make fun of him, but nothing at all would stop him. The officer said that he asked Paul if he would like him to speak to the governor about getting him moved to an open prison, but Paul said that if his Jesus could hang on a cross with His arms open wide and all those people scoffed and jeered at Him, what he was doing was nothing. The police were very moved.'

She went on to tell of their wonderful happiness together when he was released. But Paul fell sick. 'Nothing,' she said, 'could stop him talking about his new freedom. Every day he would read that Bible you gave to us – and all the magazines you still send us – but Paul grew weaker and weaker. On the last day, there in bed, looking around the room at his decorations, he was still talking about the way God had forgiven him. He's gone home now to be with Jesus – I know he has! I'm going to go on trusting Him as Paul did.'

Such perfect and complete forgiveness.

Such a story of an ordinary man who came to know the true meaning of forgiveness reminds me of the woman in the Bible who was 'forgiven much because she loved much'.

Forgiveness is indeed a beautiful word, and freely translated means 'to set free'. Jesus, our blessed Lord, was taken by cruel men, examined, humiliated, scourged and then hung upon a cross to die the death of a common felon. In the midst of His terrible suffering, He gazed on those who had placed Him there, and lifting up His head He cried, 'Father, forgive them, for they know not what they do' (Luke 23:34). In other words, what He said was, 'Father, set these people free from the crime they are committing unwittingly.' What remarkable love was expressed in this cry! Any one else probably would have cursed and called down on them all the wrath of heaven, but He, the Lord of life, opened His compassionate heart and freely forgave them.

This is the core of the Gospel; this is the 'freeing agent' which can change our daily living from a burdensome chore into exciting adventure. St Paul makes it clear in Colossians 3:13 when he tells the Church to forgive one another in the same way as Christ has forgiven them. A high standard, indeed! Is it possible to attain it? In our own strength, no! Only by the grace of God may we venture along this pathway with any measure of success, and that is what God invites us to do.

What is true forgiveness?

I was impressed by Monica Furlong's definition of forgiveness in her article, 'The act of forgiveness' in the *Church Times*, April 1977.

> We think we attain it, of course. From infancy onwards we learn from painful necessity the times in life when we must simply give way to another, because it is too difficult or dangerous to do anything else. We learn bitter lessons about siding with authority or power, or with those who have whatever it is we need most. This, however, has nothing to do with forgiveness. It is the mentality of the slave who has no option but to be compliant, since sooner or later, by hunger or pain or fear, he can be bludgeoned into submission.
>
> Forgiveness, real forgiveness, is not about swallowing down our angry emotions, but is about a free movement within us, the aim of which, is to set another free.

How often we have heard of people, perhaps ourselves, who forgive others this way: 'All right, I suppose that I have to forgive, and I do, but it'll be a long time before I forget!' They haven't forgiven at all! All they have done is to put their offenders into fetters for life. Never will they know the freedom true forgiveness brings. It reminds me of what a certain Dr Beecher calls 'Ugly Forgiveness.'

> There is an ugly kind of forgiveness – a kind of hedgehog forgiveness, shot out like quills. Men take one who has offended, and set him down before the blowpipe of their indignation, and scorch him, and burn his fault into him, and when they have pounded

him sufficiently with their fiery fists, then – they forgive him.

Could there ever be a greater demonstration of love than the liberating work of Jesus forgiving us while we were yet sinners (Rom. 5:8)? I am sure there isn't. We may experience true forgiveness and what it is to truly forgive others whenever we invite the Holy Spirit within us to bring us into a deeper understanding of the perfect forgiveness of Christ Himself. Let us never hesitate to ask Him.

Why do we experience difficulty in being forgiven?

A good question. To discover the reasons we have to be honest with ourselves, and it will help us a great deal if we avail ourselves of the Holy Spirit's assistance when the moment arrives to ask for forgiveness. Here are four reasons which I regard as important. They may prompt others to come to mind.

1. The need to believe we are right.
Some of us find it painful to be proved wrong. I remember teaching one young lady who told me that through her high school days in the U.S.A. she was taught the philosophy of never admitting to mistakes. What appeared to be a mistake, she was told, was simply a different way of interpreting a thing or action. I cannot believe there are many schools like that one. But it is a fact that many folk go out of their way to excuse or explain away their sins or failures. I think the fear arises, not so much from pride, but from a basic need to feel safe and protected. To admit the possibility of failure requires one to admit the need for forgiveness, and this may mean exposure. To be vulnerable is to be weak.

One person I know expressed it this way. 'I am a leader. If I admit failure and the need to be forgiven, then my popularity and acceptance as a leader will diminish.' If only he knew the truth. I find it almost impossible to follow happily some one who cannot admit to mistakes or failure; he is too far removed, and perhaps a little frightening.

2. *The fear of losing prestige.*

This is commonly known as the 'keeping up with the Joneses' syndrome. History shows that this has brought untold misery to many ordinary people. The tension and fear some have endured to find acceptance by peer groups is out of all proportion to the benefits. The standards set by the peer groups, whether good or bad, are to be accepted with rarely any appeal to conscience if one is desperate enough to gain admission. Unfortunately, they may interpret morality in such a manner that we are forced to hide our guilty feelings; depression soon follows.

There is only one way to be free, and that is by acknowledging our faults and failings to the Lord who understands and cares. He will help put right our lives and enable us to ask forgiveness of those against whom we have sinned, and to make any reparation. In this way we may help others who find themselves ensnared. Surely, it is worth it. To be free in the forgiveness of Jesus Christ is to come from gloomy darkness into reviving light.

3. *Fear of the consequences.*

'What will happen to me if I tell the person I have wronged him?' Surely, this has passed through our minds on many occasions. It did for me when the Lord asked me, one day, to allow Him to put my life in order. It happened in those heart-searching weeks before I came to enjoy the fullness of the Spirit.

I didn't mind getting right with God; the problem was my neighbour. God would forgive and forget, but would my neighbour? He might forgive and hold it against me for the rest of my life. I have to admit that I was very afraid of the consequences that might follow such a fool-hardy action, yet I could find peace no other way. I had to examine my heart and allow the Spirit to reveal to me the sins that were still unresolved. There seemed to be no end of them so I wrote them down on a sheet of paper. I came to realise that with God there are no small sins and no big sins – only sins.

In the days that followed I wrote a number of letters apologising to people I had hurt and asked their forgiveness. I also wrote to two firms I had worked for enclosing money in respect of items I had thoughtlessly taken. I went to my bookshelves and sorted out all the books I considered to be on 'extended loan' and returned them with notes of apology. I tried to do everything the Spirit directed, and do you know, at each stage of reparation or reconciliation, the joy within me grew. But even more importantly – and I ask you to keep this before you – not one of the people I approached turned me away, criticised me, or threatened to expose me. In fact, some expressed how moved they were by the action I had taken and desired to follow my example.

I firmly believe that the consequences of obeying the commandments of the Lord in respect of forgiving and being forgiven can only bring freedom to all parties, that is, if they enter into the exercise without any reservations.

4. The fear of rejection.

The fear of rejection is a very basic fear which plagues most of us in some way or other. We all need to be wanted; God has made us that way so there is no need to worry if we are conscious of this drive. The problem is that when we have to seek forgiveness, we have to admit our imperfect condition. Will this impair a cherished relationship or friendship? We know it shouldn't, but what if it should?

Reason it this way. If my friend knows that I have offended or hurt him, the failure to ask his forgiveness can only erode the friendship. If he doesn't know, but should discover later what I have done, then the relationship might well fall apart, or he might never fully trust me again. Either way, the true solution is confession and forgiveness. Only then can I experience lasting freedom. This holds true for any relationship. Unfortunately, the fear of being rejected makes us do some silly things to avoid being identified as the offender.

One word of advice. There are some sins of the mind that are best left to God alone. For example, a group of leaders are talking together about the remarkable things God has been doing through their personal ministries. One of the group, John X, has been ministering for only a few months and he is relating some moving experiences; everybody is applauding. I feel a tightening within me as a jealous thought arises. 'Who does he think he is going on like that?' I smile and nod my head in agreement. I mustn't allow anyone to learn what I am thinking, but I tell myself, 'I've never heard such tall stories – and everybody's believing them!'

Stop!

I must not continue! I am allowing the process of destruction to work in me! But, at the same time, I dare not tell John X what I'm thinking. It will certainly not help him nor will he be blessed with my honesty. What must I do?

I have discovered this to be an effective and healing remedy. Quietly, I confess my sin to the Lord and ask for His forgiveness. Then, I will pronounce on John every blessing I can think of that will bring him success. But I must not leave it there. I must confirm my act of repentance, and I may say to him something like this. 'John, thank you for sharing with us the beautiful things God has been doing through your ministry. Now I'm seeing you through new eyes. I want you to know that I'm going to pray for you and speak well of you. Please pray for me, will you?' This is a wonderful way to crush the spirit of jealousy. In that moment I no longer feel excluded; I am free to join myself to this group with a happy heart.

Why do we experience difficulty in forgiving?

It is important that we learn some of the answers to this question too. Listen to what Jesus said on the subject.

> For if you forgive men their trespasses, your heavenly Father also will forgive you; but if you do not forgive men their trespasses, neither will your Father forgive your trespasses.
>
> (Matt. 6:14–15)

When we fail to forgive others, we create for ourselves a blockage to receiving forgiveness from God. Our freedom to enjoy the Christian life depends on our appreciation of this truth – and acting on it.

So, let us consider four of many reasons why it may be difficult to forgive.

1. 'Why should I? He deserves to suffer!'

The answer to this reason is simple. If God treated us this way when we sinned against Him, then we would be in a very sorry state. The reason that He went to the Cross was so that we should not suffer; He suffered there for us. Therefore, should He allow us to suffer rather than forgive us when we cry to Him in our distress, He would be denying His integrity and frustrating His own plan to redeem the world.

We see then, that to withold forgiveness from anyone is to work contrary to His will and to dishonour Him. Aware of this, dare we even consider such action?

2. ' . . . but he'll probably sin again!'

No doubt at all, he will sin again – so will we! The possible recurrence of a sin must never be the reason for withholding forgiveness. Jesus made this clear when Peter asked him, 'Lord, how often shall my brother sin against me, and I forgive him? As many as seven times?' Jesus said to him, 'I do not say to you seven times, but seventy times seven' (Matt. 18:21–22).

3. 'He's not proved himself to be truly sorry!'
Please do not allow this reason to disturb you. Who can say how sorry a person is when he asks for forgiveness? What yardstick are we going to use? Doesn't the Scripture tell us that we did not pay for what we receive, therefore, we are not to make others pay for what they receive from us (Matt. 10:8b). This is one of God's principles. In the end, each one of us must answer to God regarding our honesty and motives, so until then, let us turn no one away. Let us forgive freely, rejoicing in the knowledge that we are not judges but ministers of His grace. What a privilege!

4. 'I've been hurt too much!'
Yes, this is possible. However, do not raise the shutters against the possibility of forgiving that person; our happiness depends on it. If we are wounded, then let us come without further hesitation to the Lord, our healer. There, at His side, we may rest and receive the healing balm for our souls. He is fully aware of the problem that confronts us, and He never requires us to perform impossible tasks. A person with a broken leg cannot run, a blind person cannot walk straight, and a wounded soul may find it difficult to forgive. We must learn patience. May we taste and see how good God is! Then, and only then, will we be able and confident to pour out freely on the offender the liberating blessing of forgiveness.

The convicting power of forgiveness.

When we forgive one another, it should never be our intention to humiliate or cause the offending party to suffer in any way. However, it is possible for forgiveness to bring conviction especially when there is some form of resistance.

Little Anna, aged seven years, pushed open the swing door of a Czechoslovakian police station and made her way to the sergeant's desk. She stood there waiting to be noticed with her hands behind her back clutching a small package.

'Well,' asked the sergeant, 'what do you want?'

'Please may I see the captain?' she modestly replied.

'What's your business?' came the gruff response.

'Well . . . it's about my mother.'

The sergeant lifted the telephone and dialled the captain's office.

'There's a kid to see you, sir. Something about her mother, she says.'

'Tell her to wait!' came the faint reply.

And Anna waited. An hour passed by before she dared approach the desk again. The sergeant, as if noticing her for the first time, telephoned his superior once more for instructions. In all this time she had not been offered a seat, nor had she released her grip on her package. She had just stood there waiting patiently.

At last, she was rudely ushered into the captain's office and was made to stand in front of his desk. The captain glared at her for a while wondering who she could be and why she had come to see him.

'Well!' he grunted, 'don't waste my time!'

'Please sir,' Anna commenced rather hesitantly, 'I've come about my mother. You see, it's her birthday today . . . but she's in prison. Well . . . she loves Jesus, and before she was taken she reminded me that I was always to love my enemies.'

It seemed that she was having difficulty in choosing what to say next. Plucking up courage she went on.

'You see, you are the captain who came to our house and took her away to prison. She was given three years' hard labour and she's been there a year now. Well . . .

because it's her birthday I wondered what she'd like for a present. Then I remembered what she'd said about loving our enemies . . . and so . . . I've brought you this little present.'

And with that, little Anna drew from behind her back a beautifully arranged posy of wild flowers. She approached his side, handed it to him, curtsied, and quietly left the office.

There was a long, long silence before the captain moved, and an observer noticed that his face had appreciably softened and that his eyes were unnaturally moist.

This account is true. It was reported that this same captain was transferred to another department. It seemed that he was no longer able to fulfil his duties. Many believe that God used this little child to bring this intimidating police captain to himself. What happened to him we do not know, but the report came to the West through the medium of the child and an observant, sympathetic policeman.

I am reminded of Romans 12:20, where loving and caring for our enemies is likened to 'heaping burning coals upon their head.'

Forgive – and stay free!

Unforgiveness can only produce unhappiness; our communion with God and our brother or sister is broken, the heart grows harder and inner tensions may increase with a consequent loss of joy and peace. In some instances physical sickness may result. Is it worth it? No! Sometimes, it takes a great deal of courage to ask for forgiveness or to forgive another who has hurt us but, you know, we have an obligation to God Himself who has forgiven the world's sins – and at such a price.

The closer walk with God.

Do you remember in the first chapter how we considered the experience of St John of the Cross? He could not approach God without being deeply affected by his sinful condition and his need for forgiveness. It became clear to him that the way into God's presence, the union which followed, his receptivity to His love, his increase in faith, his profound joy, all stemmed from his obedience to avail himself of Christ's forgiveness. There was no other way for him; there is no other way for us.

He invites us to draw near to Him no matter how great the sin we've committed, but remember, our ability to receive His forgiveness will depend on our willingness to forgive. We may be quite sure that He desires us to enter into the fullness of His divine life. This is real living – holy living!

A prayer to help you begin.

Lord of this world, I acknowledge with grateful thanks that you have made it possible for all peoples to receive your forgiveness and eternal life through the sacrifice, death and resurrection of your Son, Jesus. But, Lord, as I travel along this pathway before me, I am conscious of my weaknesses and sinfulness, and the many times I fall. I need your help. I need your forgiveness.

Teach me how to come to you without delay and how I need not be afraid. Impress on me the freedom forgiveness brings. Give me courage to be honest with you, myself, and with those I sin against. And Lord, I trust you to keep me from embarrassment and confusion of the enemy. You are my stronghold at such a time.

And one thing more, Lord, please give me grace to receive with warmth and openness any who ask me for forgiveness. May I freely forgive them as you have freely forgiven me. They may be nervous and unsure when they come, but may I send them away with rejoicing hearts.

Holy Lord, here I am, waiting before you. I rest in the knowledge that you will speak to me with all gentleness, for I ask these things in Jesus' Name. Amen.

11: Delighting In Our God.

So far we have been considering some of the beautiful and important truths which, if we can spend time understanding them, will enlarge our mental and spiritual appreciation of the great adventure in which we are engaged. Its success depends a good deal on how well we come to know and love the God who inspired it. By now we may see that a Christian is a very privileged person, the object of God's love and indwelling Spirit, daily being transformed into the likeness of Christ. This is why faith and forgiveness are to be priority exercises if we are to know true peace and happiness, and a close walk with God. You see, we must start drinking His life before we can bring life to others; we must be willing to receive from Him before we can give to those in need around us. So shall we take one more step in this direction and reflect on some ways in which we may delight in our good God? This is essentially giving and not asking.

The communion of lovers.

This is my definition of prayer. As a young Christian I was taught that when we prayed we were to storm the gate of heaven, wrestle with God, move His arm, and not let up until He did something. Too often I tried following this advice and ended up in a state of dejection and extreme weariness. 'Ah, Denis,' came the voice of my encourager, 'don't grow tired and give up so easily! Remember, prayer is costly!' And so I collected more prayer lists, prayed longer and harder, fully convinced that this was the way to the heart of God. Many years later I came to realise that too many people had surrendered this form of prayer for the five minutes in the morning or evening. They just could not sustain the strain. Let me try to put prayer into a New Testament perspective.

Prayer is the intercommunion between the Father and His children, and is based on an ever-developing love relationship. Sometimes it is verbal and sometimes it is non-verbal, but it is a communion which never ceases day or night. Even when we are not conscious of praying our spirits may continue to commune, but I feel certain that it is more precious to the Father and more beneficial to us when we pay attention to what He is saying so that we may offer Him a loving and filial response.

If only we would always remind ourselves that He is far more willing to commune with us than we are with Him. We need never force Him to do what He purposes to do. What He desires is that we learn what His will is so that when we pray we are participating in His will. The more we know His will, the more natural our prayer life becomes, and the more relaxed we are in His presence. Of course, this does not imply irreverence or presumption – far from it! Communion between two people who love one another can produce only increased confidence and trust; this leads to obedience. If only we would grasp the fact that God is not subject to the limitations of man. If only we would view Him in all His greatness, majesty, might and power, then, perhaps, we would cease treating Him like a man. Do you see what I mean? Understanding these truths can change our prayer times, in fact, our whole relationship.

Delighting in His presence.

Here is a practical exercise to try, but first a word of explanation and encouragement.

151

Some Christians, I find, are a little afraid of using their imagination. They feel that to use the imagination is to permit the mind to run wild, but this need not be the case at all. When we use our imagination for the purpose of this exercise we give to God the full range of our thoughts, ideas and knowledge in such a way that He is able to take them, add to them the spiritual content and correction that suits His purposes, and then interpret them to the mind in such a manner that they become meaningful to us for edification and blessing. Of course, what we see, for example, the things of heaven, need not be identical to what God sees. Most of what exists in the realm of the spirit cannot be understood with the mind – there are no adequate terms of reference for interpretation. Although we know so little about the nature of our spirits we may reasonably assume that God ministers to our consciousness through them. If what He desires to say to us will be difficult to comprehend then He may resort to parables, types, images and so on. We must with humility leave it to Him to choose how He will speak or reveal Himself to us.

A word of encouragement. This is not an exercise to determine your spirituality. Take it slowly and enjoy every moment of it. Quite possibly, at the beginning you may enjoy only some of the first four stages. That's all right. You are not trying to prove anything. Move on to any other stage at your leisure. Remember, we are individuals with differing abilities to use our imagination, so let's be ourselves.

1. Preparation.
Find a quiet place and a time when you are unhurried. If you are a mother and these times are rare, find a time when your children are most relaxed and invite them to join you. Explain to them that you are going to imagine a journey to the home where Jesus is, and would they like to join you. Let them sit near to you so that you are close to each other.

2. He is our peace.

Be relaxed, comfortable and still. Close your eyes and gently put away all thoughts but those of Jesus. He is with you because He has promised never to leave you or forsake you. He longs for you to draw near to Him because it is His joy to shower blessings on you. Listen to Him say to you, 'Come to me if you're tired; come and rest for a while. Drink in my peace and know the warmth of my presence.' Enjoy to the full this special moment of meeting. Don't hurry! The cares of the day are passing away, and from the centre of your being a spring of happiness is rising and bubbling over. Thank Him. Welcome Him. (As we move along do share what is happening with your children. Allow them to share with you what they feel and see. You will be amazed.)

3. We are joined to Him.

Now slowly bring your hands together, and as you inter-lock your fingers, say aloud something like this. 'Just as my hands are being joined together so have I been made one with my God. He has made me His forever. And as my fingers are interlocked so has He intertwined me to Himself with the bonds of His love.' Gently squeeze your hands to awaken in you the awareness of how closely He holds you to Himself. Really enjoy this time, and whisper to Him your love response. No profound prayers, please! Simply love-talk only.

4. He is our life.

Let your hands rest for a few moments on different parts of your body, you arms, your head, your trunk, your legs, and whisper a prayer similar to this one. 'Your holy life is actually in this body of mine! You really live in me, Jesus, by your Holy Spirit! This body which I am touching is a temple in which you live! What a privilege! Thank you, Lord! And what is so wonderful, Lord, is that I'm joined to all those who now live in the heavenly places. Your Spirit in me is the same Spirit who lives in them. I am never separated from them. We are one for all time.' Meditate on these truths for a while.

5. *We worship Him.*

Now slowly raise your face heavenwards. Keep your eyes closed but imagine you are opening your spiritual eyes. What do you see? Think for a moment of what you know about heaven. Look around you; you are viewing by faith the hosts of heaven. Think! The Holy Spirit who fills God's kingdom above is at the same time quickening in you!

There are the countless angels and archangels in varying splendour. These attendant beings wait to fulfil the least wish of the invisible God. And there are the saints both small and great whose garments are of whitest white and whose voices now fill the heavenly vaults with songs of joyful praise. Their names are written in the Book of Life; no more the pain and suffering they bear for they have overcome through the blood of the Lamb who now appears. See, He is standing there for all to see – for you and me to see – His holiness as blazing light, the marks of His triumph still visible on his hands, and feet, and side.

Spend as much time as you wish taking all this in. Allow your heart to worship from a distance at first.

Now look and see if you make out His face. Renew the thoughts of what He has done for you, personally, and then look again. Through the splendour you may grow aware of His perfect humanity. He is identifying with you. The details of His face will be different for each one of us – according to how we know Him. He has such a lovely face; it is so noble, so strong, so gracious, yet so compassionately gentle.

And now He smiles – yes, at you! He is so glad that you've come. See, His arms are outstretched to welcome you – as if you are the only one there. Don't be afraid! Come nearer, and as His love flows out to you so receive Him with a thankful heart. How approachable He is.

154

The glories of all heaven pale into insignificance as you meditate on such a holy yet acceptable countenance. Breathe your prayer of joyful surrender to His divine will.

You are now sitting in humble adoration at His feet. Nothing matters any more because you are where you've always wanted to be. You are dwelling in the realm that is timeless; no longer is there a need to hurry – so rest – drink deeply. His presence floods your being with vision and with hope. He speaks your new name, a name inextricably interwoven with His glorious Name, the knowledge of which is too wonderful for it is the fullness of divinity and excellence, and yet . . . and yet, you hear its echo as you taste the sweetness of such sublime intimacy. How can you express that which transcends all human understanding? All you can whisper is, 'My precious God, I love you!'

All too soon the moment is gone, but not the wonder, and not the certainty that He is even more vibrantly alive in you. Intercession reaches new depths of meaning, and service changes from duty to delight.

A final word. Don't be discouraged if what I have described is not your experience. Yours may well be a different one. However, learning is a process, so don't give up. One thing is certain, you will never regret having tried.

Delighting in Him through the Bible.

The Bible is another means of delighting in Him. This is not the study of the Bible for the sake of understanding God's plan and purpose for mankind, which is a vital exercise, but a means of discovering His person and presence.

I find it a great help to read books about the background of Bible incidents, such as, how people lived in Jesus' day, how they dressed, the work they did, what was the geography of the country, how they travelled, the social and political conditions at a particular time, and so on. There are some very helpful and reasonably priced books available today to help us.

Now because our access to God is through Jesus, I use the Gospels more than any other book in the Bible because we have a more direct contact with Him there. As before, we invite the Holy Spirit to help us use our imagination and knowledge aright. Perhaps it will be helpful if I share with you how we might interpret a passage of the Scriptures; let us say, the healing of blind Bartimaeus in Mark 10:46–52.

1. Preparing ourselves.

It will be best to choose a time of day when there are few interruptions and find a place where we will be alone. Our prayer might follow these lines. 'Dear Lord, here we are with you. Please make this passage from the Bible come alive so that we may see you and come to know you better. We believe that you will do just this. Amen.'

We should read, then, the passage selected three or four times, reading it two or three times from, say, the Living Bible or some other modern version. With each reading we should try to absorb the details so that, finally, we can paint a mental picture of the scene, the characters and the action. Finally, we review the effects of the story on us.

2. Preparing the scene.

We are standing outside the main gate of the city of Jericho looking at its heavy sun-bleached walls capped with vantage points for the sentries. On either side of the two huge gates and adjoining the walls are the watch towers that house the guards and also serve as the offices for the city officials. Small houses and shops of the poorer folk litter the edges of the road into the city, and through these buildings we see at intervals fields and clusters of trees worked by the tenant farmers. To the east, the land rises to Jerusalem, while to the west, there is clear evidence of the great Jordan valley terminating in the Dead Sea.

It is April and a warm pleasant day, and like any other busy city it is full of comings and goings; the noise at times is deafening. Amidst the scores of common folk we can see the strutting city official, the imperious off-duty Roman soldiers, the haughty elder of Israel with robes drawn closely around him to avoid contamination, the elegant courtier, and the merchants with their camel trains or mules kicking up great clouds of dust. There are shopkeepers, hawkers, rabbis, scribes, bankers, slaves, housewives and children, the crippled, the dumb, the outcast, the beggars – and the blind. One particular blind person we see there, resting his back against a broken wall with one hand clutching his begging bowl and the other hand raised to ward off the indifferent kicks from the passers-by. From where we stand we see opulence, arrogance, greed and indifference mingled with poverty, brokenness, despair and helplessness – and we see in this blind man such loneliness. His name is Bartimaeus.

3. Seeing Jesus.

Few can realise the desperate plight of the blind like Bartimaeus in Jesus' day. He had to fend for himself in every possible way; he was almost an outcast. As such, he knew only helplessness and hopelessness. He was a nobody and the crowds he mingled with treated him with the minimum of respect. But, somehow, Bartimaeus had heard of Jesus.

He lifts his head and turns his sightless eyes towards the city gates. The sounds have changed; everyone is hurrying to join the crowd now emerging from the city. The blind man rises to his feet. He has waited, oh so long, for Jesus to come his way. He reaches out a hand to stop a child. 'Tell me,' he cries, 'is it Jesus?' The child looks into his face with pity and replies, 'Yes, it's Jesus!' but the pull of the crowd is too great, he leaves the blind man standing there and runs to join it. Bartimaeus dare not let this moment pass; his life depends on it! Look at him! Nothing will stop him attracting Jesus' attention. He's shouting for all he's worth.

'Jesus, thou son of David, have mercy on me!'

See the way the crowds are trying to stop him. But Bartimaeus is now a determined man and he is letting them know that nothing at all is going to stop him from reaching Jesus. He shouts again and again. He waves his arms in the air; no one can fail to see him!

Wait a moment; the crowd is stopping; they're falling silent. That must be Jesus in the centre. What a gracious person He is. His eyes blaze with anger at those who have tried to stop the blind man calling to Him, but a moment later, as He turns His face on Bartimaeus, they are filled with utmost compassion – I think they are moistened by tears.

Yes, this is the beloved man of Galilee; no wonder the common people hear Him gladly!

Do you see? Jesus is calling the blind man; He has eyes for no one else. And now look at the crowd; they can't do enough for him! But Bartimaeus knows their fickleness and is throwing aside his coat and pushing his way through them to Jesus. The relief from years of suffering and rejection shows on his face as he falls down at the feet of Jesus.

4. The face of God.

And Jesus? . . .

We are looking into the face of God in perfect man; a face which expresses strength and nobility, a face filled with tenderness and infinite mercy. No deceit or guile is there for He is the embodiment of truth and righteousness. The light in His eyes brings hope to the hopeless, and the words of His mouth are life and healing to the weary and broken. From His heart flows forgiveness to the repentant sinner and restoration to the outcast. Who can resist Him, who can fail to surrender themselves to

Him? He opens his gracious arms of love to accept all of us – even as we are – no one is ever turned away.

And now, He gazes on broken, destitute, blind Bartimaeus – and loves him.

'What do you want me to do for you?' He asks.

'Master, please let me receive my sight,' comes an almost whispered reply.

This is the moment of truth as the liberating heart of the Father in heaven releases through His Son, Jesus, unlimited healing for body, soul and spirit. He speaks the word, and it is done!

'Go your way, your faith has made you well!'

Now look at Bartimaeus! He's received his sight indeed! His eyes are opened wide! He sees! He's looking full into the face of his Redeemer; what he sees and has received has transformed him into a willing disciple.

Can anything be more wonderful or exciting? Isn't it worth spending as much time as possible meditating on this deeply moving experience and the effect it has on us so that we may delight in God with a full and thankful heart?

There are so many more wonderful incidents in the Bible like this one to consider.

Other Scriptures.

If you should select, say, a teaching Scripture, try to bear in mind that you are not so much concerned with good exegesis as getting to know our Lord personally. Make every question you ask direct you to Him. Take for example, 1 John 4:8b.

'God is love.'

1. *God*. – Meditate on some of the meaningful things you know about him: His all-powerfulness, His all-knowingness, His ever-presence. Marvel at the works of His creation, such as the universe, the starry heavens,

the earth and the beauty of its covering. Consider His personality and His character, or His glorious plan for redeeming mankind. There are so many things, so don't hurry.

Now meditate on these truths as they relate to you. This is your God, the one you serve and honour. He is completely in control of all things, the world around you, the events of your life. Nothing may happen without Him permitting it. Spend time being happy with Him and be thankful.

2. . . . *is love*. – Consider! This God not only loves, but IS love! If He lives in us, then love is living in us. We may love with His love. This love is the same love which allowed His Son to take our place on the Cross. It never varies or changes in any way. Learning about this love is a process where each stage will lead us nearer to God.

Now sit back and rest for a while. God is loving you right now; He never ceases loving you. This love is transforming you and deepening your awareness of Him. It seems almost too wonderful to be true, doesn't it, that this great and glorious God on whom we are meditating has condescended to enter our humanity?

'God is love' ceases to be just a familiar Bible text but a love message from Him to us – and this is how it should be.

Delighting in God through the things around us.

I remember waiting for a bus in Limehouse, London, and like some buses, it was a long time coming. So I spent those waiting moments contemplating the drab high-rise buildings and the equally drab assortment of business premises. There was not a tree or a patch of green to be seen anywhere. I wondered where God was in all this – but He *was* there. Behind me was a low wall, and at its base I noticed a tiny island of living things. I bent down to examine it and to my amazement I counted fifteen kinds of plants and creatures. There were tiny plants I could not name, two or three sorts of grass, mosses, a dandelion, two snails, a black beetle and numerous ants. It was beautifully self-contained and quite oblivious to the world at large. And I thought to myself that this was the work of the same wonderful God who made the universe.

The truth is that we may see the hand of the Creator everywhere – if we look with enough care. Delighting in God springs from observing through all the senses what He has made, and then allowing His Holy Spirit to interpret His message of purpose and love to our hearts. We must not be afraid of using our senses to the full whenever we can for they are His gifts to us. As we delight in the gifts of sight, hearing, smell, taste and touch, so we should delight in the Giver who is ever present.

When next you take a walk through the local park or your own back garden, if you have one, take a deep breath of the good fresh air. There is so much of it and you'll never be wanting for the next breath. Isn't that something to be thankful for? Perhaps you will smell the newly mown grass, or the border flowers, or the mixed fragrances of the shrubs and trees, so evocative and enlivening. And count, if you can, the varieties of flowers, both wild and cultivated, each owning a peculiar fragrance, shape and colour. Carefully feel the subtle and differing textures of the petals and leaves, and mark the complex arrangement of the stamens and carpels, and then ask yourself whether you can remain silent in the light of such revelation. Surely, your heart must cry, 'Lord, who is like unto thee?' Gratefully delight in the good God who has given us all things to enjoy.

For God so loved the world . . .

Did you know that God doesn't love Christians alone (although Christians are usually more able to receive his love)? He loves every man, woman and child living on

161

this planet, Earth. Unfortunately, the majority of mankind is hampered by the confines of industrial and city life and hasn't free access to the treasure of the countryside and beautiful gardens. But I want to tell you something to encourage you. We may turn this disadvantage to our advantage if, when we seek to delight in God, we observe and consider the pinnacle of his creation, namely, people. Yes, I mean those teeming hordes with whom we may do battle on the buses and the trains, or in the supermarkets or football stands. Is this difficult to believe? It is a fact that we are daily mingling and living with the most wonderful of God's creation. And what is more, He is truly at work in them even if they do tread on your toes or knock over your shopping bag.

People watching.

Not so long ago I sat in an underground train taking me to Kings Cross in London and I tried to look at the busy, bustling crowd around me through God's eyes. To be sure, I witnessed rudeness, anger, aloofness, misery, greed, hopelessness, and many other evidences of a wounded world. However, I observed too some delicate shafts of bright revelation from a hidden sun. I noticed the protective arm of a young mother around her little daughter and the smile that passed between them. A young lad, somewhat confused because of his mates, offering his seat to an elderly man. Two middle-aged ladies recounting the fun they had experienced shopping together for the first time in years. There was the courteous response of the black guard who addressed the tramp-like man as 'Sir'; the encouraging smile of the business man for the meek little spinster lady who looked so lost. There was so much more and I felt my eyes growing moist. It was rather like looking into the face of Jesus and hearing Him say, 'Denis, you're beginning to catch a glimpse of what meaningful life is all about.'

It fills me with hope when I consider what the Church

of Christ can become (let alone the world), if every Christian were to engage in this mental and spiritual exercise instead of finding fault or degrading his neighbour. Our hearts would grow more tender with every passing day, our joy to love and serve Him increase, and above all, Jesus, our blessed Lord, would be reflected in our shared life.

'Take delight in the Lord . . .'

The full text of Psalm 37:4 is 'Take delight in the Lord, and he will give you the desires of your heart.' One nineteenth-century commentator makes this observation when considering the word 'delight'. He says, 'It is a very forcible word, which, however, inadequately expresses the feeling of blessedness and rapture in the original. The true counterpoise to envy of the temporal prosperity of the wicked is the inward intensity of joy in communion with God.'

I have come to realise now that delighting in the Lord, whether through meditation, Scripture, observing His creative works, or any other suitable way, is rather like walking a pathway which leads to His heart. Let me explain what I think happens.

Whenever we give ourselves to delighting in God we invoke the aid of His blessed Spirit who helps us to enter a state of, what I call, spirit-awareness. This is a very gentle process and it allows our spirits to drink at the fountain-head of Truth and Life. Our mind-awareness is restricted because of what I feel to be an inadequacy on the part of the spirit to communicate with the mind. Our facilities for interpretation are severely limited by reason of the differing natures of the mind and the spirit. Nevertheless, some important communications are made which awaken in us a consciousness of God's will and His everlasting concern for us. What He desires for us to do, and to become, take on new significance and meaning, and this desire of His works in us to become the desire of our heart – we long to do His will. We can say, with reasonable assurance, that delighting in the Lord encourages the process of transformation of our beings into His likeness (Matt. 17:2; Rom. 12:2; 2 Cor. 3:18).

Who can resist such an invitation to love and to be loved? You do not have to be a great Bible student or theologian, neither do you have to be wise or clever, nor need the approval of any human being. Too many of us are struggling to maintain our Christian composure, and sharing the message of Christ's life lacks integrity and vitality. Listen anew! The voice of the Spirit and the Bride may still be heard. It says to all who long for that closer walk, ' "Come," and let him who hears say, "Come," and let him who is thirsty come, let him who desires take the water of life without price' (Rev. 22:17). Can any invitation be more personal, more promising, more filled with longing?

'Come, my children,' says the Father, 'and delight yourselves in me.'

A prayer.

O Lord God of heaven and earth, you have seen my weariness and loneliness in my search to know you better, and I have come to the moment when I can go no further. I have tried to find you and to serve you in my own strength – and I've failed. Please forgive me? I thank you.

With all my heart I choose to be yours in body, mind and spirit. Here I am with nothing to offer you but what you have already given me. I sincerely pray that your blessed Holy Spirit will be my friend, my teacher, my intercessor, so that I may grow in the knowledge of your Son, Jesus Christ.

Teach me how to wait on you, how to see you in the Scriptures, and how to see you in all the works of your creation. Above all, help me to surrender myself to you in such a way that I may have the great joy of delighting in you. My soul longs to be joined to you, Lord God, fused into you, loved by you, so that, one day, I may be thoroughly transformed into the likeness of your Son.

With a glad heart I accept your invitation to come, and I accept it through Jesus Christ, my Saviour. Amen.

12: Chosen and Called of God.

Perhaps by now we are beginning to understand the meaning of holiness. It is the gentle process of being conformed into God's likeness. As we learn to give ourselves to receive His love like little children, as we delight in Him, so we are transformed. This enables us to offer Him the service of our love which is life-giving to those around us. True love for God must find its outlet in practice, otherwise it remains but an ideal or a dream.

Here is an example of living holiness in a group of people I know.

Living holiness.

'Denis! You've arrived safely!' That's Sister Elizabeth. 'Come in, will you now, we have your meal waiting.'

Handshakes, smiles and more warm welcomes from the other sisters before I'm installed in the convent guest room. It is simply furnished but I notice the loving care that has gone into its preparation – the flowers, the bowl of fruit and chocolate biscuits, the bed turned down, and the little card of welcome. Later that evening we will pray together and then I'll listen to all the happenings before the personal prayer times.

Where am I? In one of the many Convents of the Presentation, a remarkable Catholic order founded by Nano Nagle in 1775 to reach and minister to the desperately needy of Cork in Ireland. Needless to say, the work has grown since those days with sisters serving in teaching, nursing, or some sort of social work, reaching many countries of the world. Then what makes it so special? It is simply that these sisters endeavour to live their lives according to Miss Nagle's God-given vision, which is caring – caring for all no matter who they are or what their needs might be. Whenever I have the privilege of visiting them I see this corporate, caring heart in their lives, their activities, and especially in their worship, and I am deeply moved.

But caring consistently with joy and patience is so very different from caring when the mood takes us; we all know that. So what is their secret? It took me time to realise the answer for these sisters are very human, have a good sense of fun, have their ups and downs like most of us, and know the meaning of vocational crisis with its depressions. I discovered the answer in their attitude to God and His will. To put it in one word, they were 'surrendered,' or 'given'. Yes, that's what is was. I don't suppose for a moment that they would admit this truth but my belief was confirmed whenever I listened to them talk, around the meal table or sitting together in the lounge after a hard day's work. They talked of their retreats or special days of prayer with warmth, of their need to know Christ better, of their longing to share their faith with those they taught or nursed, and always in an atmosphere of simple humility and happiness. They were real people, approachable, with many imperfections by their own admission, but their warmth and love, I could see, was because of their honest and ever-developing relationship with God. This, to me, was living holiness.

The meaning of holiness.

It is a fact that when we talk about holy things in the Bible, we are talking about people or things usually set apart or separated. We also understand that they are set apart by a person for a particular purpose. In a special way that thing or person becomes different. We may not see this difference but it is there all the same.

When we use the word holy in connection with people and God there is another factor always to be taken into consideration: it is the response of the person who is called and set aside. Like the Presentation Sisters, he must be willing not only to be set apart, or separated, for a special purpose, but he must be prepared to give himself wholeheartedly to God who calls him. I use the word wholeheartedly because we may make promises to God, or even take vows, without actually giving our hearts. It is us He wants, not our accomplishments or personal gifts, although He will receive these if our hearts are first surrendered.

Listen to some of the Scriptures on the subject of God calling us.

Do you not know that your body is a temple of the Holy Spirit within you, which you have from God? You are not your own; you were bought with a price. So glorify God in your body.

(1 Cor. 6:19–20).

. . . present your bodies as a living sacrifice, holy and acceptable to God, which is your spiritual worship.

(Rom. 12:1b)

. . . but as he who called you is holy, be holy yourselves in all your conduct, since it is written, 'You shall be holy, for I am holy'

(1 Pet. 1:15–16)

(God)..who saved us and called us with a holy calling, not in virtue of our works, but in virtue of his own purpose and the grace which he gave us in Christ Jesus ages ago.

(2 Tim. 1:9)

When I first read such Scriptures I was sure that God

was expecting too much from me; who could live to such high standards? It depressed me for I was well aware that my weaknesses outweighed my strengths and there was little hope of any immediate change. But God did not leave me to my own devices. Through the years He worked in me a change which, at last, enabled me to see, firstly, that it is more enjoyable and natural to be holy as a Christian than not to be. Secondly, it is through the life of holiness that we make ourselves available to the free flow of God's sparkling life, grace and energy. It is rather like Peter who had to move out and away from the boat before he could really experience walking on water. God calls us to holiness but we have to give ourselves to becoming holy in order to enjoy the freedom and happiness it brings. It would seem that His greatest longing is to bring mankind into His closest embrace.

But isn't this difficult to accept without question?

Holiness and suffering.

Two or three years after I had commenced my Christian walk, I experienced a growing concern to enter the ministry. I had little idea what this entailed, but thirty or forty years ago this was interpreted to mean ordination into the regular ministry or missionary service. I had hoped, secretly, that God had had the former in mind for me but I had that sneaking suspicion that He would manipulate my reasoning until I accepted a call to some primitive and distant country of the world as a missionary. Wasn't it taught in good church circles (and perhaps it still is in some today) that to serve God you must be holy and know how to suffer? I am not denying that a servant of God must be holy and that he will meet suffering on the way, but I interpreted the inference to mean that the more you served, and suffered as a consequence, the holier you became. But how could this be if it is God who makes us holy? Why, even the giving of ourselves to this holy life must precede anything He

169

calls us to do or undergo. Well, God was to make me a wiser man.

An unusual missionary call.

What led me to believe that God would ultimately call me to missionary service was a peculiar and almost uncontrollable desire to attend missionary meetings. I couldn't stay away from them. If I remember correctly, the first I ever attended was in 1953. It was one of the annual gatherings of the Mission to Lepers and was held at the Friends' Meeting House in London. The details escape my memory but the effect the missionaries' reports had on me disturbed my complacency. I heard of their privations and hardships, of successes and failures, of broken lives changed through love and care, and of their faith in a compassionate God who never failed them. Who were these remarkable people – these missionaries? They had to be another breed of Christian, for surely, no ordinary people could perform such tasks with such dedication. My answer was forthcoming.

The chairman stood at the close of the meeting and moved to stand before the lectern. He bowed his head in prayer, looked up, and addressed the gathering. 'Tonight,' he said, 'I'm not appealing for money, and I'm sure that you do support us in prayer. I am calling for men and women who will offer themselves to work among the lepers in any part of the world. You know the price to be paid, but I would point out that this call comes from our Lord and Master who has given all for us. You will not go in your own strength but in His. I cannot press you into service, and I will not. I simply ask you to consider the privilege.'

Silence.

'Now,' he continued, 'If you have made a decision, come now to the front and kneel here on this step.'

My heart was thumping. I tried to appear as if I was giving the matter much thought, but the truth was, I was peering through my hands which covered my face to see who could be bold enough (or should I say, foolish enough) to make that dreadful journey to the front. But they came – four of them – two men and two women – and they knelt.

Well, there was my answer. But who would have dreamed that anyone could be called to missionary service in such an unusual manner.

'My child, I desire to love you!'

I left the Friends' Meeting House that night in confusion. What had happened to me? I felt anger rising within me and I couldn't be sure of the true reason. I blamed the chairman for being so presumptuous. He should never have cornered those four volunteers the way he did; they didn't stand a chance. That would be the last missionary meeting I would attend. But three days later I was scanning the advertisements in the Christian press for other meetings. Surely, I was losing my grip on reality!

Nearly every week I attended a missionary meeting or conference. I did not realise there were so many societies; over one hundred and thirty non-Catholic and over one hundred Catholic. Looking back over those years I think I must have developed a love-hate relationship with them. I would assimilate the details of the reports, even talk to the missionaries when possible, but I could never bring myself to making any kind of positive response. Secretly, I told myself that God was calling me and that if I didn't do something about it He would chastise me – but I was too frightened to do something about it! Could all this really be of God or was it my imagination working overtime? I had to know. The answer came almost two years later at a local Sudan Interior Mission meeting held in a parish church in South London.

Three missionaries on leave had given their reports of the happenings on their stations and, as is often the case, each had emphasised the urgent need for more workers. They had to be people fully committed to God, they said, for there were many hardships to face and not a few dangers. I felt sick within. I wanted to run and get well away from the place but I simply couldn't move. I had discovered by now that personal calls for service where intending missionaries could offer themselves openly occurred only now and again, but that night, I had a strong premonition (or was it the look in the speaker's eye) that he would make such a call – and he did!

'Why not make a public declaration of your intention and come forward to the altar rail and kneel?'

I could sit there no longer. I had to move – but to the front? Could I do it? But I was on my way with others following me.

I remember the frantic calls I made to heaven as I walked. 'Lord, where are you going to send me? Please don't let it be China! I think I can make a go of it in Africa – but never China!' Then I thought to myself that it was a foolish thing to do to tell God where you don't want to go because that is surely where He'll send you. That had been firmly impressed on me. So, I blotted it out of my mind until I found myself at the altar rail. Now wait for it! How exactly did God tell you where to go? Some missionaries I had spoken to said that they heard a sort of inner voice. Would I hear an inner voice – and how would I know it was God?

Nothing happened – not a whisper! But I felt so happy kneeling there. He would surely tell me where to go when I arrived home. Yes, that was it! Still nothing from heaven. 'Lord, is there something wrong? Is my hearing at fault, or something? Please tell me what you want of me?' Truly, I was perplexed but I revelled in my new sense of freedom and closeness to Him.

A whole week passed. No voices; no indication at all concerning my future. That night I knelt by my bed and prayed to Him like a little child. 'Lord, forgive me if

I've created problems for you. I feel so relieved now that I've offered myself to you but I'm still at a loss to know where you want me to go. Lord, is it Africa . . . or is it even China? With your help I'm sure that any place in the world will be acceptable. Please do put my mind at rest. Thank you, Lord.'

Then, I heard the clearest, gentlest and confirming of voices. It seemed to come from deep within me filling my heart and mind with quiet certainty. 'My child,' God said, 'I do not want you to go anywhere at all. Think very carefully and you will see that it was the only way I could reach you to love you.'

The way to the Father's heart.

What a blessed truth this is. If only we would feed on its substance how different things could be. Unfortunately, we are conditioned by the world to believe that acceptance depends on what we have to give, or to put it another way, you get nothing unless you pay for it. Then we allow God to take charge of our lives and He tells us that we are loved for who we are and not for what we can do. This 'works syndrome' results in too many Christians experiencing considerable inner conflict which drives them to acknowledge with enthusiasm the doctrine of grace, while at the same time, working hard to demonstrate their worthiness of this grace. Please understand that I am not denying the need for good works, the Scriptures are abundantly clear on this matter, but I am saying that if our priorities are right, then priority number one will be for us to surrender ourselves so fully to God that He will be enabled to pour His love on us as He desires. This profound love will stimulate in us a responsive love which will then produce the true works of holiness.

The works of holiness.

Perhaps it will be helpful at this stage to consider a little more carefully these works, but first, let us briefly summarise the main truths in this chapter.

1. Priority number one is for us to surrender ourselves as fully as possible to God's love.

2. This love will stimulate in us a responsive love from which holy works may proceed.

3. This life of holiness enables us to receive more freely the blessings God desires to pour on us.

4. It is easier for a Christian to live a holy life than to live a selfish one. There is an agreement between the indwelling Christ and holy living which removes tensions and fears.

5. Learning to live this life is a process and takes time. It requires a mental readjustment from the works syndrome.

6. Our standing before God is because He accepts us through the sacrificial work of Jesus Christ, His Son, and not because of anything we do (other than believe).

I think you will see that if we use these six truths as our foundation then the holy works we do must originate from the One who calls us and makes us holy, God Himself. As we have observed in a previous chapter, He communicates His will and purpose through the agency of the Holy Spirit, but if we are to be intelligent participators, having the same mind as His, then we need to know the reasons why and how. Remember, we are not slaves but active sons and daughters.

Why holy works?

Ephesians 4:3–6 presents the case for holiness most beautifully.

> There is one body and one Spirit, just as you were called to one hope that belongs to your call, one Lord, one faith, one baptism, one God and Father of us all, who is above all and through all and in all.

The Apostle here is not simply talking about the unity of God, but essentially, about the unity of God with His Church, or His body. As He is one so we must be one with Him. This wholeness, oneness, completeness of the Church, this unity in faith and action, is a declaration of intention on God's part to the whole of creation. He desires all men to be saved – made complete, joined to him – for such is His love and such is the redemptive work of His Son (1 Tim. 2:3). And so, as we learn to live lives of holiness, identifying with Him through the givenness of ourselves, so God's blessed invitation is seen more clearly and understood more fully. You could say, that the Church today is a twentieth-century incarnation of the Christ, which, in turn, means that each of us must ask the question of ourselves, 'Am I so given to my Lord tat His unity shines through my life so that others are drawn to Him?'

The single ultimate purpose of God is to make all things one with Himself (Rev. 5:13). This is a more than adequate reason for allowing His Spirit to produce in us works of holiness, don't you think? There is a sense of urgency in verse 3 of Ephesians 4 which reads in the Amplified version, 'Eager, to make effort, to be prompt or diligent, to maintain the unity of the Spirit in the bond of peace.'

How good works should be done.

1. Right attitudes.
Ephesians 4:1–2 puts it succinctly. It says:

> I therefore, a prisoner for the Lord, beg you to lead

a life worthy of the calling to which you have been called, with all lowliness and meekness, with patience, forbearing one another in love.

You could say that this is the reconditioning process necessary for holy living. Some people say that they cannot change, and never will. That is rather like shutting the door on God. Of course, we cannot change ourselves, but we may change our attitudes, and we can give ourselves to change. Keep in mind the fact that although it is God who makes us holy, and we have to give ourselves to becoming holy, the outworking of the process through the operation of the Holy Spirit will take a lifetime. After some consideration we may see that the qualities of lowliness, meekness, patience, and forbearing in love are the essential ingredients which shape our character so effectively that God's plan, outworking in us for unity, becomes exciting and very uplifting. For some this may be difficult to believe until we allow it to happen. We must take it on God's word that it will. These steps may be helpful to follow.

(a) Take a look at the person you are. Be honest with yourself. Are the qualities of lowliness, meekness, patience and forbearance alive and growing in you? If they are not, admit it!

(b) Acknowledge your own inability to effect any reasonable change. You need God to help you, so tell Him everything, the problems you experience, the weaknesses you feel.

(c) Cultivate a listening ear to His still small voice. Take courage from the Scriptures. Remember, you are not the only one with your difficulties. Sharing with others can be helpful.

(d) When confronted with the need for lowliness, meekness, patience and forbearance – STOP! – you are about to make a decision! Invite the Holy Spirit to help you make the right one. He will! Now act.

(e) Change takes time. Don't be afraid of failure or

making a mistake. These could be sure signs of growth. Always give thanks.

2. *The gifts and grace of God.*

> But grace was given to each of us, according to the measure of Christ's gift,
>
> (Eph.4:7)
>
> and his gifts were that some should be apostles, some prophets, some evangelists, some pastors and teachers.
>
> (Eph.4:11)
>
> Having gifts that differ according to the grace given to us, let us use them . . . in our serving . . . in teaching . . . in exhortation . . . in contributing . . . in giving aid . . . in acts of mercy.
>
> (Rom.12:6–8)

In 1 Corinthians 12:27–30 even more gifts are referred to, while in 1 Corinthians 12:4–11, special gifts of the Holy Spirit are listed.

We can be sure that Jesus, who was full of the Holy Spirit, had all these gifts – and He used them freely. Now these gifts are not to be thought of as commodities which are sent down from God in boxes, duly labelled and addressed, to those who ask for them. Try to see them as activities or operations of the Holy Spirit who lives within us. In principle, each of us has all the gifts for the Holy Spirit is a person and cannot live in us in part. He is fully in me and He is fully in you. Needless to say, because each of us has a rather different calling, each of us will use a different variety of gifts, with one or two of them being quite prominent. Together, we are the revelation of Christ alive in the world today.

One final thought. Whatever our calling, whatever our gifts, let us do everything through His grace which is boundless. The way of our Saviour is the true path of holiness and is expressed so eloquently in the Gospel of St. John.

> Truly, truly, I say to you, the Son can do nothing of his own accord, but only what he sees the Father doing; for whatever he does, that the Son does likewise. For the Father loves the Son, and shows Him all that he himself is doing.

(19:20a)

You may like to use this prayer:
Holy Father, I long to be able to pray the prayer of your Son, Jesus. I desire to do nothing of my own accord but only what I see you doing. However, at times, I feel a long way from even discovering the pathway of true holiness. Yet, I know this cannot be, for you have promised to live within me – and you do.

Now, from a sincere desire to be fully yours, I give myself anew to you. My happiness depends on my giveness and this is a process I must learn. Teach me your ways, dear Lord. Show me the beauty of your face and draw me with your love.

Teach me too the way of lowliness, meekness, patience and forbearance in love. Make me accessible to your divine grace. Let me be a holy vessel for your Spirit to live in so that I may be truly united with you and with your body here on earth and in heaven.

And, holy Lord God, shine through me so that others may see your beauty, and your heart be satisfied. Thank you for your compassion and great patience with me, through Jesus Christ, who is forever faithful. Amen.

13: Drinking the Water of Life.

At the close of the Book of Revelation there is a strong, moving invitation to all who will listen. It reads:

> The Spirit and the Bride say, 'Come'. And let him who hears say, 'Come'. And let him who is thirsty come, let him who desires take the water of life without price.

> (Rev.22:17)

In a way, this is what this book is about. Holiness means coming to the water of life, drinking freely, and staying there. This fount, this spring, this source is Jesus, and as we have seen, we come by the way of the Cross. As we grow into His likeness from day to day, so we discover something of divine love's transforming work for we are being changed from one degree of glory to another. God has called us into a remarkable, new relationship as sons and He has given to us His blessed Spirit to be our closest companion and friend. No wonder a faith that binds us to Him, and a forgiveness that frees us to love Him, generates in us the heart's urgent need to delight in Him. He is everything a person can want; He supplies everything a person can need. Is it not reasonable and right to be given to such a Lord? We might well pray:

'Yes, Lord, with all my heart and soul I desire to dwell in your secret place and drink forever of your pure water of life.'

Freely receive His life.

The only prerequisite for drinking freely of this water is thirst. We may avail ourselves of it as much as we need and as often as we like, and there is an unlimited supply. It is God freely giving Himself to us in every possible way. Remember, He gives us nothing unless He wants us to have it, and He gives it because He knows we need it. Therefore, the best way to honour Him is to receive all of it with expectant and thankful hearts. This makes Him glad – and that is a good thing, isn't it? And so, if we are thirsty, and we should be, let us come and take of this wonderful water of life and never cease drinking it.

Now may I suggest that we consider how this water of life comes to us from God, and then, how we may promote the receiving of it.

Revealed through His Spirit.

About three years ago I was preparing a Bible study when, to my joy, I was challenged by the Scripture, 1 Corinthians 2:7–10. It reads:

> But we impart a secret and hidden wisdom of God, which God decreed before the ages for our glorific-ation. None of the rulers of this age understood this; for if they had, they would not have crucified the Lord of glory. But as it is written, 'What no eye has seen, nor ear heard, nor the heart of man conceived, what God has prepared for those who love him,' God has revealed to us through the Spirit. . .

St Paul is excited as he tells his readers of what lies ahead of them. They are destined for glory, the nature of which is impossible to describe. Never has there lived a person on earth who has seen anything resembling it. Never has a person existed who has heard anything to compare with it. No, whatever it is that God has prepared for those who love Him has not even been conceived in anyone's heart.

Then St Paul makes this remarkable statement. In the vernacular of today he might have put it this way. 'Now listen everybody, and listen very carefully, for what I am about to tell you will astonish you. Can you believe that what God has prepared for those who love Him, has in fact, been revealed to us through His Spirit!'

I feel sure that had I been privileged to have been there I would have made my way to him afterwards and said, 'Please, Paul, what, exactly, has been revealed to us – to me? I want to know!'

Speaking mysteries to God.

This Scripture in 1 Corinthians 2 led me to consider afresh an aspect of speaking with tongues recorded in 1 Corinthians 14. There, it clearly states that it is not edifying or helpful to use this gift in a church service without an interpreter being present to interpret (v.5); there must be no confusion. On the other hand St Paul encourages all to speak with tongues (v.5), for when we do so we are speaking mysteries to God in the Spirit (v.2). Of course, we are talking of private prayer. Can we understand what we say when we pray this way? The answer is no, we cannot. Verse 14 says, 'For if I pray in a tongue, my spirit prays but my mind is unfruitful.' I have heard some people remark with cynicism, 'If I can't understand what I'm saying, then, what's the use of it?' I would reply to this question by saying that if through speaking in tongues I am speaking mysteries to God, and St Paul was an expert in this art, I want to go right on using this beautiful gift for it has been given to me by God. I would rather not be the person to tell Him that He is wrong.

Revelation to our spirits and to our minds.

These two Scriptures, together with many others, helped me to appreciate that God does communicate to our spirits profound mysteries and that our spirits may communicate mysteries with Him. I have often wondered what it is we are saying to each other. My guess is that it is impossible for the natural mind to grasp more than a fraction of such revelation and truth because it is mostly spiritual in content and communicable only at the level of the spirit. Romans 8:26 tells us that, 'the Spirit himself intercedes for us with sighs too deep for words'. This must be a twenty-four hour a day activity as far as God is concerned although its substance is outside of space and time. It transcends most known forms of communication; it is deep calling to deep. In this realm of the spiritual there are no adequate terms of reference to help our minds fathom the riches of God's mysteries. And yet . . .

And yet our minds are not left high and dry; He is concerned that we are built up in body, mind and spirit, and for this reason He employs such means as types, shadows, parables, allegories and metaphors, to communicate His message of life. When the need arises, and this does not appear to be often, He may use dreams, visitations and visions. These make a marked impact on the mind as well as the spirit. They have a propensity to strengthen our faith in the purposes of God. So many things become clearer and, what is more, they have an objectivity which allows us never to forget them. They could be said to become part of us. I will illustrate this truth.

No place to live.

Shortly after my wife, Florence Mary, and I were married, we experienced the stress of finding new accommodation. I had found a slightly better job in another part of London and it was necessary that we look for a place nearer to hand. The smallest flatlets were being let at exorbitant rents and, day by day, we were growing more desperate. What could we do; where could we go? The only answer left to us was temporary separation. Florence Mary would return to her mother in Bournemouth and I would stay with two very good friends, Jimmy and Ruth MacKenzie. They offered me their only spare room which was small and could accommodate just a single bed and my few odds and ends.

The days that followed were full of the sense of failure and hopelessness relieved only by letters from Florence Mary and the encouraging exhortations of our good friends. Where was God in all this? Surely, if He was truly God, He could find us the perfect accommodation at the drop of a hat. I did my best not to let the folk around me know what was passing through my mind although they must have detected something from my long face. I was not a very companionable person.

Angel visitors.

One night, after Jimmy and Ruth had gone to bed, I decided to spend some time on my knees before God. I was not at all sure what would be accomplished but I could not walk this path of hopelessness any longer without some explanation. Prayer had become for me the driest of exercises so that I would not have blamed God had nothing happened.

I selected the kitchen for the occasion and knelt in the centre of the room resting my elbows on a wooden chair. The bare light above me gave the room a clinical look and I closed my eyes to shut it out. But for the distant sounds of the occasional passing car in the street the house was quiet and I felt very alone. I remained still on my knees for some minutes trying to bring order to my thoughts. I wondered why my wife had to pass through such times of darkness and confusion. What lay ahead of us? More darkness? More confusion?

'What are you doing with us, Lord,' I cried.

The words had no sooner left my mouth when I became conscious of being surrounded. Gently, I raised my head keeping my eyes closed. I was certain that whoever these visitors were, they were not of this world.

If some person were to relate to me this incident which I am describing, I would ask a multitude of questions. As a matter of fact, I did ask many that night. Who were these magnificent beings? Were they real or imaginary? Why had they come – to me?

As I silently sought for answers it dawned on me that I was not at all afraid; astonished, intrigued, but not afraid. My eyes were still closed. I had not thought of opening them, but now I would. This would, surely, help to determine the objectivity of this remarkable visitation – if that was what it was.

Ministering spirits from God.

I took a deep breath and slowly opened my eyes.

They were there – angels! I could actually see them! I could not count their number without turning around but there must have been between ten and twelve of them in the form of a regular circle.

What I write now is what I believe I saw then. It is possible that their appearance was relevant only to the message they brought – I do not know. The kitchen had somehow grown in size for their circle was reasonably large but they were in no way confined. In height they were between six and a half and seven feet, and each stood in an attitude of utmost confidence and rest, hands clasped at the front and faces looking down on me kneeling there. They were such beautiful and dignified beings and the only way I can describe their faces is to say that they glowed with a golden sheen which radiated the wisdom and the knowledge of the ages. They were timeless. It was impossible to say whether they looked young, middle-aged or old as one would with human companions. As I gazed into their eyes I had a distinct feeling that I was looking into another world. I could hear no words but I was quite sure they were communing with each other, matters far beyond my comprehension. I cannot even adequately describe their robes for they were much more than coverings for the body, rather, they seemed to be expressions of their character, vibrating with life and purpose. Indeed, the whole company of them gathered there that night transformed the kitchen into a power-house.

But why had they come?

The protective canopy over me.

As I have said, I was not afraid, in fact, I seemed to absorb the peace of these wonderful beings. I was protected.

Then, quite suddenly, I found myself outside of the circle as if it was expected of me to take the role of an observer. I could see myself still kneeling with my arms resting on the chair while the angels stood guard around me. I remembered the Scripture in the book of Hebrews where it tells us that they are ministering spirits sent forth to serve for the sake of those who are to obtain salvation (1:14). How privileged we are!

As I continued to watch another change took place. An almost inpenetrable darkness was seen to cover the angels, but this darkness could not draw nearer, nor could it penetrate an invisible dome-shaped canopy suspended over them. Darkness had met with light but darkness could not overcome it (John 1:5). At this stage I could see nothing of what the darkness held, but I could feel it in my spirit as a dark, hideous deception which sought to devastate me and to divert me from the course approved by God. From every quarter and with every ounce of energy unseen forces flung themselves at me, but as they made contact with the invisible canopy, they themselves were hurled back into their own darkness. Gradually, I perceived their grotesque forms and I noticed that some were darkly beautiful; they were more devious in their attack. But I took courage and hope rose within me as I noticed that at no time were the angels distracted from their task of watching over me. Not a tremor shook them as these powers of darkness sought access to my kneeling form through the circle of protection.

I was safe – Florence Mary and I were safe! No matter what trials and tribulations would come our way, such as finding a place to live or making ends meet, we could be assured that if we walked God's perfect way in his strength, no powers of darkness could touch us. We will slip and fall if we turn from looking into Jesus' face to consider the might and power of the enemy, but remember, the only power he has over us is the power we give him!

Making ourselves available.

As I have said, visions and visitations are rare. Perhaps we may never receive one. However, I do know that my particular experience was like the window of heaven being opened to me. Spiritual certainties relating to God's steadfastness and love, as well as to His provision, were the life-giving water I cried for at that time. I came to Him without anything to offer as payment, and He gave me drink. My attitude of mind was extremely negative and I still wonder why He graciously ministered to me this way. It certainly shows how bountiful and merciful our God is, doesn't it? He is full of surprises.

Freely receiving.

Perhaps, at this stage, it will be helpful to consider some simple exercises that will allow us to make ourselves more available to the life-giving water from our heavenly Father. I am sure that you have experienced those times when God seems to be so far away, and what makes the matter worse, you cannot muster up even the beginnings of a thirst. What do we do then? Wait and hope? No, I do not believe that God abandons us, but He does wait for us to offer ourselves to Him no matter what state we may find ourselves in.

Now when I speak of exercises I do not mean pray more, study the Bible more, or put more effort into serving. It is much more than that. It is rather a matter of allowing Him to possess us, so that we in turn, assimilate His life and character.

Allow me to share with you how I, personally, attempt to put this into practice. You may find other ways which are just as helpful.

1. The Bible.

When I read my Bible there are times when I try not to read it in order to increase my knowledge of what it contains. With the help of the Holy Spirit I set out to meet in a personal way the one who means so much to me – Jesus. Through Him I will see the Father. This we discussed in the last chapter.

I select a passage that is not too difficult to understand, perhaps, a miracle or a healing, or an aspect of Jesus' life. When I am comfortable and rested, I read it through three or four times, and then meditate on it verse by verse. Then conscious that the Spirit will help me, I allow Him to bring the passage to life in my imagination so that I see everything that took place.

My imagination quickened, I see Jesus talking to his disciples, or to the crowds who have come from far and near to hear this gracious teacher. I try to capture the intonations of His voice, the movements of His hands, the benevolence of His smile; all those wonderful characteristics that make Him so approachable and desirable. I spend time looking into the faces of His listeners; there is wistfulness, there is the smile of hope, there is the grimace of pain, there in the silence they sit spellbound. And when He rises to minister to their physical needs, how can I not be moved by their cries of joy as the wounded and the broken receive the healing touch of His firm but gentle hands?

Yes, this is the mighty God, who through the blessed Christ, is quickening my spirit and opening my eyes to who He is. This is drinking the pure water of life, transforming water, invigorating water; water that will never run dry.

Take your Bible and allow it to become for you a source book for living.

2. Worship and praise.

This spiritual exercise is not confined to churchgoing on Sundays. I am sure you are aware of that. Throughout the day we may enjoy the pleasure of worshipping Him and praising Him, but there is nothing quite as intimate as those times we set aside for this sole purpose.

I have found it helpful to use one of the praise Psalms in the Bible. Once more, with the aid of the Holy Spirit, I sit quietly with my eyes closed meditating on what I have read. I focus my attention and imagination on, say, the majesty, might and power of my God who, in fact, defies description. I whisper with care His names, allowing the meaning of each to sink in. I drink in the effects. No need to hurry! I consider, in the light of what I know, the magnificent redemptive work of Christ, His Son, marvelling at each stage of His journey from heaven to earth and back again, where, to the loud acclaim of the welcoming angel hosts, He takes His place at His Father's side. I revel in the nature and character of this holy Lord of mine, overwhelmed that He could love me enough to prepare a place for me in the presence of His Father. I usually find it too much for my finite mind to take in. All I can do is to sit quietly and worship Him and praise Him for His goodness. Then, when all words cease to do Him justice, I fall silent and allow myself to bathe in His presence. This is sometimes like sitting in the sunshine and opening to its warmth like a flower. I am drinking in His life and I am glad.

I should add that quite often I only reach the second or third verse of the psalm. It doesn't matter. This exercise is to help us drink in God's life-giving water. Of course, there are many other passages of Scripture you can use.

And one final word. I do want you to understand that I do not always achieve these goals. I have my ups and downs like anyone else, but of this I am certain, I am seeing the pathway of worship and praise more clearly as I dare to walk it. Some of us may feel that we are passing through this world like strangers in a dry land. If this is so, then all the more reason to seek and enjoy the rivers, springs and wells God has provided along the way.

3. Jesus – the ever-present friend.

A Christ-like disposition to daily living is more than living out our lives in a way that seems to please Him. Let me explain what I mean. If, as we have seen, God is transforming us into His likeness, if He loves us to the extent that we are made His sons and daughters, and if His Spirit has come to dwell in us, then surely, it is reasonable to suppose that in every waking moment we may be conscious of Him living His divine life through us. Personally, I see it as a matter of developing this consciousness of Him, relating to Him through the day as we would a close friend. The problem is that we cannot see Him, so it is often a case of out of sight, out of mind. What do we do then? The answer seems to be that we must cultivate new habit patterns.

We must allow our friendship with Him to deepen. We must try not to take Him for granted. Learn to discuss the day with Him, where we are going and what we are going to do. If we ask a question of Him or seek

His guidance, give Him the opportunity and time to answer. It need not be verbal. More often than not it takes the form of an inner prompting or persuasion.

Then, as we considered in the last chapter, let us delight in all the good things we see around us. The blessings of nature: trees, flowers, the blue sky above, the sun with its warm rays, and so many other wonderful gifts that we, too often, take for granted. Be thankful for everything, the sound of laughter, the welcoming smile, the kind deed and the generous act, friends and loved ones.

Cultivate the habit of seeing everything through Christ's eyes, listening to those things that please him, rejoicing when we see good and mourning when evil is done, or when people suffer harm. Let us develop a sensitive nature so that whatever He says or does we may desire to co-operate with Him.

Nothing is more exciting and liberating than this ever-growing knowledge of His living presence within us. This is one of the many delightful ways in which God is able to stimulate our thirst for him.

Knowing Jesus is everything.

If I have laboured too much on knowing Christ's living presence, it is for a good reason. This conscious indwelling enables us to know what His perfect will is, and therefore, how to interpret the Scriptures in terms of His promises. He becomes such a close friend that doubting His integrity is painful to us, and having faith in His promises is a natural response. We begin to understand why it is written, that 'without faith it is impossible to please God' (Heb.11:6). Growing in faith is such a gentle process and the benefits are enormous. Growing up, receiving His love, being transformed, becoming a child of His, and knowing the fullness of His Spirit, are all experiences of faith in His promises. We must permit the truths we have shared to take root in the heart, mind and spirit, and we will never regret having embarked on this remarkable journey of life.

Here is a prayer to summarise our thinking and desires now that we are at the close of this book.

Lord God, we thank you for binding us to yourself with the cords of your divine and perfect love. Keep ever before us the truth that this love extends to all mankind, and that you desire all to enjoy the gift of eternal life. To this end and for your good pleasure may we learn daily how to live in your holy place, to yearn for the eucharistic food and drink which is your self to us. And so, being clothed with your righteousness may we reveal to this world through our lives and service the living presence of your Son, Jesus Christ.

Lord, our sincere desire is to drink of the water of your life so that we may grow in boldness, purity and love. Let us never be ashamed of our faith in you, so that when you appear, we may be found truly acceptable.

And so we honour you, blessed Trinity – Father, Son and Holy Spirit, and we ask for your covering and protection as we go out into the world. All these things we humbly ask in the high Name of Jesus, our Lord. Amen.